P9-DSZ-377

DATE DUE

~~JAN 9 '97~~			

Inka
Dinka
Doo

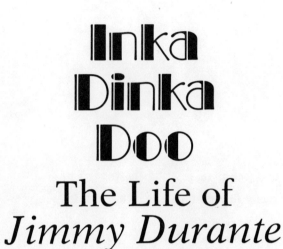

Inka Dinka Doo

The Life of
Jimmy Durante

JHAN ROBBINS

Paragon House
New York

First edition, 1991

Published in the United States by

Paragon House
90 Fifth Avenue
New York, N.Y. 10011

Copyright © 1991 by Jhan Robbins

Designed by Jules Perlmutter/Off-Broadway Graphics

Manufactured in the United States of America

Library of Congress Cataloging-in-Publication Data

Robbins, Jhan.
    Inka dinka doo: the life of Jimmy Durante/Jhan
  Robbins—1st ed.
      p. cm.
    Includes bibliographical references and index.
    ISBN 1-55778-418-3 : $19.95
    1. Durante. Jimmy.   I. Title.
  PN2287.D87R6   1991
  792.7'028'092—dc20
  [B]   91-15305
                                                 CIP

To the memory of
Charles D. Rice

Although he and Durante were long time friends, Schnozzola would become confused when introducing him. Then he'd remember that Charlie's last name had something to do with grain. "Meet Charlie Wheat," Jimmy would say cheerfully. Sometimes it was "Charlie Oats" or "Charlie Rye" or "Charlie Barley."

Contents

Contents

Acknowledgments

I'm indebted to Steve Allen, Don Ameche, Milton Berle, Father Charles Boland, Ernest Borgnine, George Burns, Pat Buttram, Sid Caesar, Roy Campanella, Anna Capalbo, Marlene Dietrich, Joe Franklin, Dr. Henry Goldsmith, Carlos Gonzales, Kathryn Grayson, Bob Hope, A. E. Hotchner, Betty Hutton, Van Johnson, Loretta Lambert, Peggy Lee, Janet Leigh, Bernie Lewis, Father Daniel McManus, Robert Mitchum, Garry Moore, Donald O'Connor, Mildred Plowden, Martha Raye, Ronald Reagan, Mickey Rooney, Frank Sinatra, Margaret Truman.

A special note of gratitude to David Fisher for his constant helpful advice; PJ Dempsey and June Reno for their editing; researchers Frances Rafferty and Barbara Ackerman; Polly Brown for her typing. My final words of appreciation go to my wife, Sallie Prugh: "Thank you for your support, suggestions and patience."

Preface

When Jimmy Durante died in 1980 at the age of eighty-six, he took his outsized nose, gravel voice, fractured language, and penguin strut with him. The stage trademarks made him, probably, the most recognizable performer of his time. "We got a million good lookin' guys," the live Pinocchio would say. "But I'm a novelty."

Durante performed in the era of Ragtime, during World War I, the Roaring Twenties, Prohibition, the Depression, World War II, the Kennedy Years, and Vietnam. His story is a museum of show business—vaudeville, nightclubs, Broadway, movies, radio, and television. Jimmy's wistful "Goodnight, Mrs. Calabash, wherever you are" as he walked away from the fading footlights will be long remembered. There were many stories regarding the identity of Mrs. Calabash, but she remained a mystery. His long lasting appeal wasn't—he got to your heart.

Despite his "moiderin'" the English language with his "deese" and "dem," you joyfully accepted his often difficult-to-interpret linguistic style. His old friend, George Burns, often commented about Jimmy's unique manner of speaking. "Schnozzola," he'd say, "is the only person in the entire entertainment field who isn't terrified of working live. After all, if he said anything wrong, how could you tell?"

I got to know Durante well. We planned to collaborate on his life story. It never came off because he was always too occupied to sit down for long periods. "I'm up to my heels in workin'," he'd apologize. Whenever I'd manage to take some notes, Jimmy would pretend to frown. He'd shout, "How many times I got to tell you writer guys, it's the kiss of debt to put it down in ink! Say it with jewels, or flowers, even drink! But never say it in ink!"

During our proposed book project I talked to many people who knew Durante intimately. Among them: Eddie Jackson, Billy Rose, Jack Dempsey, Walter Winchell, Harry James, Phil Silvers, Abel Green, Ed Sullivan, George Raft, Quentin Reynolds, and Eddie Cantor. They all lauded him. When I told that to Jimmy, he'd become indignant. "I'm mortified!" he'd say belligerently. "I demand a recount! They must be thinkin' of some other guy!"

They weren't. Fortunately, I kept my notes. When I reread them there was no mistaking the praise. In preparation for this book I once again spoke to many of his friends—those who are still around. I found they continued to feel that way or even more so.

We first met in 1953. At the time I was writing an article about him for *This Week*, a magazine that was distributed on Sundays by leading newspapers. During the interview we discovered that my grandfather had his hair cut by Jimmy's father, Bartolomeo Durante, who owned a barbershop on Manhattan's Lower East Side. My grandfather's tonsorial habits put me in solid. "That there fact makes you *meshpucha*," Jimmy said. *Meshpucha* is the Yiddish word for family. Although he was Italian, he frequently used Jewish expressions.

It didn't seem to matter that our ages were far apart. "Maybe it's because I got the brains of a little kid," he said. "They didn't grow. Only the nose. An' now I thank God for that. But I still keep wonderin' why people pay all that money just to hear me. Let's face it, my gags ain't so hot."

He may have been right. No one else could get away with

the old joke: "I put a slug in a slot machine an' what do you think comes out? (pause) The manager!"

On stage he appeared to be constantly baffled by a crazy, mixed-up world. To punctuate his rage, he'd hopessly slam his ragged fedora on the floor. When he tried to put it back on, a pile of dust would fall out. "I'm surrounded by assassins!" he'd yell with mock dismay. "The boss of this joint is too stingy to hire a sweeper!"

You may have listened to those standard lines a dozen times, but to hear them again from Durante was like meeting an old friend. He saluted a joke with a happy, "I got a million of them." Over the years Jimmy kidded the owners of the places he performed in, he kidded the waiters, the musicians, the customers, the cooks, and the doormen. During Prohibition days his audience often included notorious gangsters but even the most hardened criminals rarely objected to the gibes he aimed at them. His satire always left his "victims" happy and beaming. They seemed to agree with description Gene Fowler, an early Durante biographer, had given him: "Half-hooligan, half saint."

I heard that characterization repeatedly as I talked to people who knew Schnozzola. Due to the staggering book advances paid these days for personal memoirs, it's become increasingly difficult to interview leading entertainers. Most of them want to keep all colorful material for their own use. However, the moment I mentioned the name of Jimmy Durante, they lit up and fondly looked back.

Frank Sinatra, often a two-fisted hermit when dealing with writers, was typical. He was eager to talk about Durante. "Schnozzola would tell me that not only did I sing through my nose but that sometimes I was off key," Sinatra said. "I'd flatten guys for less. Not Jimmy. Him, I just hugged. There was something about him that never made you angry. I remember the time Bing, Dean, and myself planned to make a movie about his life. Dean was to take the part of Durante. It never came off. 'That's fine with me,' Jimmy said when he found out. 'I need somebody that looks more dashin' an' handsome like me. Maybe Errol Flynn or Clark Gable?' "

Durante wasn't a singer like Sinatra any more than he was

a comic technician like Bob Hope. He lacked the polish of Johnny Carson, the bluntness of Humphrey Bogart. When malapropisms and errors were deliberately inserted into his scripts he would mispronounce the mispronunciations. Other entertainers squeezed laughs out of vulgarity but not he.

Then what was his secret?

Born on the Kitchen Table

" 'Holy Smokes!' yells da neighbor lady whose deliverin' me. 'Dis ain't da baby, it's da stork!' "

Durante frequently used the anecdote in his act. It always produced laughs, but there was some truth to it. After slapping the newborn's buttocks, the midwife attempted to soothe the startled parents. She tried to assure them that babies quickly change appearance for the better. "In my particular case she was a hunnert-'n-ten percent wrong," he'd tell the audience. "Because of my looks, I had to go through life carryin' a interior complex."

He inherited his sizable nose from his mother, Rosa, a mail-order bride who had emigrated from Salerno, Italy, in 1886. Her husband-to-be, Bartolomeo Durante, also a Salerno native, was living in a Brooklyn, New York, boarding house. His landlady showed him a picture of her sister, Rosa, who was anxious to find an Italian-American husband. They corresponded. A year later he sent for her.

Bartolomeo had learned the barber trade in Italy; but, before his departure to the new world, he had to agree to work for eighteen months as a laborer for a construction firm that was building the Manhattan Third Avenue El.

1

Obviously, he was the victim of a corrupt practice that was very common at the time. Unscrupulous labor contractors realized that thousands of impoverished and illiterate workers fleeing Central and Eastern Europe were eager to get "free" transportation to America. It was only when these immigrants arrived did they discover what they had signed. In 1894, a Greek witness appearing before the U.S. Immigration Commission testified, "I so wish to come here that I sign anything. Then I learn I sign to be an almost slave." Despite impassioned statements like this one, the chattel operation continued to exist for several decades.

To earn extra money Bartolomeo moonlighted as the company's night watchman. "Even though Pop used to work two shifts," Jimmy said, "he was still pretty sharp-eyed. He told me that in all the time he was watchin', they never stole a single girder off him."

When Bartolomeo's period of servitude was over, and with the help of his new wife's dowry, he opened a barbershop in the Ridgewood section of Brooklyn. In rapid order the Durantes had three children: Michael, Albert, and Lillian. After Lillian was born, the family—and the barbershop—moved to 90 Catherine Street on Manhattan's Lower East Side. It was the most populated area in the country and also the poorest. President Grover Cleveland had recently called it "The nation's worst slum."

Cleveland was commenting on a report he had read: "Crime, filth, and disease make up the trio that dominates that plagued neighborhood of newly arrived immigrants. Rancid tenements line the crowded streets. It is not uncommon to find a family of ten or more living in two tiny rooms. In the stifling heat of summer when being inside becomes unbearable, the family fights for space on the fire escape. Shriveled old men and women sit forlornly on the broken front steps. In the winter everybody huddles together for warmth. The dimly lit halls smell of urine or worse. . . . The only saving grace is that one can't sink lower."

Soon, Rosa was again pregnant. Unfortunately, the baby was stillborn. Her next two attempts resulted in miscarriages. Their new neighborhood had one of the highest infant mortality rates in the country. A short time later Rosa discovered that another child was on the way. This one survived. Since the Durantes lived in three exceptionally small rooms behind the barbershop, Ethel Carelli, the midwife, chose to use the kitchen table.

James Francis Durante was born on February 10, 1893. That morning a man named Harrison Schermerhorn held up buggy and bicycle traffic on Broadway as he recklessly drove his new self-propelled three-wheeler horseless carriage at the "breakneck speed" of fifteen miles an hour. An electric taxicab was introduced to the wide-eyed public. Its owner, the Electric Vehicle Company, proudly announced that a dozen more would soon be available to pick up customers. Also on that day, New York Bell Telephone Company ran an advertisement that boasted they already had fifteen thousand subscribers and that these lucky customers were able to make long distance calls to Washington or even to Chicago.

Theodore Roosevelt, then a member of the U.S. Civil Service Commission, was asked to comment on the ad's jubilant message. He told reporters, "An infant fortunate enough to be born in this decade will surely experience miracles."

The new Durante baby was baptized at St. James Roman Catholic Church on nearby Oliver Street. Father Thomas L. Garland, who conducted the service, had to shout to be heard above the raucous cries of pushcart peddlers hawking old clothes, homemade pasta, and knishes. From early morning to well past sundown, they could be heard in a variety of languages. Blind and deaf beggars were found on each corner. Grimy store windows covered by thick black drapes shielded "social club" members from curious eyes. The streets were littered with garbage. Rats and roaches were taken for granted—everyone had them.

I once asked Jimmy about his childhood. If his being reared under such circumstances had left any emotional and psychological scars? He shook his head vehemently. "No!" he said. "It was mostly a good one for me. We wasn't what you'd call poverty-stricken. Sure, all of us kids had to help out by workin', but this don't mean we don't have enough to eat or was always cryin' our eyes out. In lots of ways, I was a very

3

lucky kid because my brothers and sister, God rest their souls, always liked me a lot."

Two of them, Albert and Lillian, indicated that affection to a reporter from the New York *Telegram*.

Albert: "My job was to take care of him when he was little. One day, me and Jimmy went to a park that was pretty far from our house. Jimmy wandered away. He must have been five or six at the time. I searched and searched but couldn't find him anywhere. A lot of kidnapping was going on, and I thought that was what happened. Or maybe he had drowned in the East River which was very close to where he lived. Suddenly, on Houston Street there he was eating a charlotte russe.* A lady had seen him looking sad and out of pure sympathy bought it for him. Even when he was very little there was something about him that made you want to do something nice for him.

"I remember one time he let the bathtub overflow. It was in the kitchen and everything got soaked. Pop was real sore and started to take off his belt to give Jimmy a couple of whacks. What does the kid do? He put his hands on his hips, hung his head, and looked terribly downcast. Then he said, 'Am I sad!' The way he said it made us start laughing. Pop the loudest. I don't think he used the belt on Jimmy that time."

Lillian: "Jimmy was pretty young when we moved to a bigger apartment down the block on number 1 Catherine Street. He didn't like the idea very much although it had steam heat and an inside bathroom. So when the moving men came to take away the furniture, they found Jimmy pretending to be sound asleep in bed. No amount of yelling and shouting could wake him up. Finally, he opened his eyes and acted surprised. 'What's all the yelling about?' he asked innocently. 'A fire or something?' He inherited my mother's sweetness and my father's talent. You know, in the old country, my father once worked as a barker in carnival. . .

---

*A popular New York confection in the early 1900s—sponge cake encased in a round cardboard holder and topped with whipped cream and a maraschino cherry.

"One Easter Sunday, Papa borrowed a horse and wagon that was used for carrying ice so he could drive us up Fifth Avenue. All of us kids piled in the back as he kept shouting orders to make the horse go faster. Along the way we passed lots of fancy mansions and people wearing stylish clothes. Many of the ladies were leading French poodles that had been clipped very close and carefully groomed. Those animals seemed to be the only thing Jimmy was interested in. Every time he'd see one, he'd say, 'Poor doggie. Bad lady!' In all the time we were growing up, I never heard him say anything stronger than that."

In 1899, at the age of six, Jimmy was enrolled in Public School 114. "Kids ain't supposed to remember that far back," he said. "But for me it's like it happened yesterday. I was wearin' a white shirt an' a blue tie. Mr. Herndon, the school principal, patted me on the nose. My mother didn't speak English so good, so she kept mostly still. But I could tell she didn't like his touchin' my nose. I did the interpertin'. Shame on me when I told her he made me a monitor right off. She believed me and kissed me in front of everybody. At the time we were livin' in the fourth ward. A kid would come up to you an' ask you what ward did you live in? If it was the same as his, it was okay. If it was different. Brother—fireworks!

"But it was a great neighborhood. Near us was a kosher butcher store. It was owned by Mr. Berman who wore a red-headed wig that kept fallin' off. His son, Marvin, was in my class. Me an' him used to do everythin' together. The other kids used to call us, 'The Bologna Boys.' "

Jimmy was obviously enjoying recalling the past. His very tiny eyes became even smaller as he reminisced. "Yeah, me an' Marvin had lots of wild times," he said. "It's a miracle we never winded up in jail. Marvin became a top surgeon. In World War II, the British government decorated him for savin' hundreds of lives."

A favorite game was shoplifting in the local five and dime store. The declared winner was the youngster who was able to safely pocket the most items without being caught. Patrick Henry Wang was usually the victor. The Durante's house was on the fringe of Chinatown and several Oriental youngsters attended Public School 114. "Patsy was a funny kind of combination," Jimmy said. "His father who owned a restaurant was Chinese. His mother was Irish. None of the other kids wanted to play with him. Not the Irish or the Chinese. Nobody wanted him, so we let him hang around with us. Patsy was the littlest kid in my class. Little an' skinny. His head didn't even reach the top of the counter. That's why nobody could see what he was doin'."

The Lower East Side's new arrivals would show appreciation of their adopted country by staging mammoth celebrations on the Fourth of July. "We used to have bonfires taller then my house," Jimmy recalled. "Street fightin' and shootin' guns, an' big parades. I remember the time Mr. Berman, the butcher, gave me a big firecracker. But it wouldn't go off, so I start blowin' on it. Suddenly, I hear a big bang. My brother, Michael, took me to the hospital. A doctor said it's a wonder I didn't go blind, but it missed my nose. We also celebrated the Feast of San Genero. For that, there'd be dancin' in the street, an' cookin' outdoors if the weather was good. The men would get loaded on lots of beer, especially my father. He'd kiss every girl in the entire neighborhood. Those were happy days."

That's the way Jimmy remembered it, but told me that he regularly suffered the taunts of his classmates. "I hardly ever went to school full time," he said. "I quit for good when I got to the seventh grade. It wasn't I couldn't learn. No, I think the real reason was the kids would yell, 'There goes big nose!'"

One of the boys who mocked him the most was known as the Whale because of his tremendous size. During recess he'd constantly ridicule Jimmy's nose. This would lead to fist fights which the Whale always won. "It gets so bad that I wish he'd die so he'd let me alone," said Durante. "I get the wish when one summer he goes to visit his uncle on a farm an' gets killed in some kind of accident. For years I felt I wished it on him an' would wake up in a sweat from dreamin' about it.

"Once, everybody in my class goes for a boat ride an' a girl says to me, 'If I should fall overboard by accident, promise you won't try to save me. I'd rather drown then be saved by someone who looks like you!' "

Jimmy noticed my pained expression as I listened to his school days recollections. Hastily, he ceased being so solemn. In all the conversations I had with him—and they were many—he rarely complained. The moment he realized that he was sounding downbeat, he'd grin and offer a wisecrack. "Save that girl?" he said. "Why, I could hardly swim!"

I once asked him how he had acquired his positive outlook on life. He was puzzled for a few seconds and chewed his ever present cigar. Then he laughed. Not loud. Not long. "Positive outlook on life?" he repeated in a kind of amazement. "Maybe my father was the one who gave it to me," he finally replied. "Pop would say, 'They just jealous! Look at your mother who has a big nose, too. An' didn't I marry her? How lucky could she get? So there's room for every person in the world. No matter what!' "

Because of overcrowded conditions, Jimmy was in the school's afternoon session—11:30 to 4:30. Approximately two-thirds of the children attended public school. The remaining third was enrolled in schools that were run by the local parish. Rosa Durante, who was the most religious member of the family, wanted to send Jimmy to parochial school, but her husband was against it. "It's not just the money," he said. "In America everybody goes to school with everybody!"

"The public school was bad enough," Jimmy said. "You had to wear a white shirt an' a tie. But the other kind was even stricter. The sisters made you shine your shoes every single day and put fancy covers on all your books!"

After the final bell rang, he'd pick up a bundle of newspapers and sell them in front of City Hall. There, he'd outshout his competitors. One of his regular customers, Bryan Murphy, a New York City alderman, commented about the youngster's loud voice. "To me it was signal," he said. "When I'd hear it, I knew it was time for me to take my pill."*

---

*Some years later, Bryan Murphy tried to convince Tammany Hall that he'd be a good candidate for mayor. Despite Jimmy's vigorous support he failed to get the nomination.

7

On Saturdays, Jimmy was required to help out in the barbershop. Many of the customers were Tammany Hall politicians. For years he kept a nickel tip Al Smith* had given him. "In those days," Jimmy said, "men still took lots of outside shaves. Sometimes the shop was so filled up with customers that some of them had to wait outside for their turn to come. In the summertime, my mother and Lillian would hand out cold lemonade while they waited."

Jimmy's chore was lathering faces before Bartholomeo applied the razor. Michael and Albert had previously had the lathering task, but now held other jobs—Michael in a photo-engraving firm, and Albert, a six-footer, joined the police department. He tried to convince his younger brother that he, too, should consider a police career.

"I liked Al a whole lot," Jimmy said. "I didn't want to hurt his feelin', so I told him I'd think about it. But I could tell it wasn't for me—I wanted to be somethin' else. Besides, my father hoped I'd become a concert piano player like that Russian guy, Sergeant Rockinoff."†

* Alfred E. Smith was born on the Lower East Side, a few blocks away from Durante's boyhood home. Although Smith was closely associated with Tammany Hall he became an extremely vigorous and popular New York State governor—he served four terms. In 1928 he was nominated for President on the Democratic ticket. "But he lost out to Herbert Hoover mainly on account of he was Catholic like me," Jimmy said. "There was lots of mud throwin' on him because of his religion. An' that ain't a nice thing to happen in this country."

† Sergei Rachmaninoff.

2

Ragtime Not Rachmaninoff

"**I** think what I am today is because of my father," Jimmy once told a Las Vegas radio interviewer. "Even though Pop always had very strict old country ways of actin' to us kids, he made a great impression on me. Like what he believed in an' the things he did."

Bartolomeo, who lived to be ninety-three years old, was a neighborhood character. If he liked you, he'd cut your hair for free—that is, if you appreciated opera music. His favorite was Enrico Caruso singing *I Pagliacci*. He kept a victrola in the barbershop, and played phonograph records throughout the day. When a customer complained, he'd be kicked out.

Although Bartolomeo retired at the age of seventy-five, he continued to give haircuts. He would carry his barber tools in a small briefcase and stop shaggy-haired strangers to offer his services. One of them was swimming champion and film actor, Johnny Weissmuller, who had purposely let his hair grow for a Tarzan movie role. "Mr. Durante was about to start snipping," said Weissmuller. "I managed to stop him, but it wasn't easy. He sure was a determined man."

Another idiosyncracy was Bartolomeo's passion for raw eggs. "It's good for the health," he claimed. A drawer that contained his razor and scissors also stored a supply of fresh eggs. He passed on that enthusiasm to his son. An item in Ripley's *Believe It or Not* feature said: "Jimmy Durante eats two raw eggs every day."

"It was the honest truth," Jimmy said. "When I see what it does for Pop, I decide to do the same thing an' it works for me wonders. Maybe you think I don't got too much hair on my head. Well, don't be sorry for me." With great delight, Jimmy patted his few remaining hairs. "Every one of those strands got a muscle," he said. "An' it's all because of those raw eggs I eat. My father knew a lot about how you should make yourself strong."

Jimmy insisted that Bartolomeo was the first person to advocate weight lifting for good health. "It starts when neighborhood kids take to stealing the barber pole," he said. "Sometimes they'd hide it on the roof of Mrs. Perina's house or tie it to a telephone pole. Places like that. But instead of gettin' sore or hittin' them, Pop would make those kids carry it back. Then he'd make them lift the barber pole up an' down for a hundred times."

In addition to Bartolomeo's strong views on music and muscle, he frequently spoke out against intolerance. "Pop was always tellin' us how we had to be fair to everybody," Jimmy said. "Except for people who wore green bow ties. For some reason he didn't trust them. Don't ask me why?"

Bartolomeo was particularly aroused when two Italian immigrants were scheduled to be executed. Pictures of them were prominently displayed in the barbershop window. It was alleged that on April 15, 1920, Nicola Sacco and Bartolomeo Vanzetti, admitted anarchists, murdered the paymaster and guard of a Braintree, Massachusetts, shoe factory. The crime had occurred during the Red Scare following World War I and the Bolshevik Revolution in Russia. At the time a large part of the public was inflamed over supposed alien subversion and demanded "100 percent Americanism." Police arrested Sacco and Vanzetti. They were brought to trial before bigoted Judge Webster Thayer who privately referred to the defendants as "dagos" and "anarchist bastards." He allowed the prosecutor to exploit the Communist hysteria. Despite very flimsy evidence, the two men were found guilty and sentenced to death.

The case became one of the most controversial legal battles in our country's history and was responsible for huge demonstrations throughout the world. The question of the men's guilt may remain in doubt, though not the bias of the court. The belief persists that Sacco and Vanzetti were executed for their political beliefs and ethnic background. Although they went to the electric chair on August 23, 1927, Jimmy's father refused to remove their pictures. He had made his beliefs so widely known that government officials questioned his patriotism. "Nothin' ever came of it," Jimmy said. "Pop was no Bolshevik. He just felt sorry for people. *'Giacoma,'* he'd say. 'Maybe we ain't born so equal, but everybody die equal!' "

Another story that Jimmy relished telling was the time his parents went for a vacation to Staten Island, then one of New York's new boroughs. It was not until 1898 that New York City became greater New York. Under a new charter from the state legislature, the city reached its present size—five boroughs united under one mayor. Before then, New York City consisted only of Manhattan and the Bronx. Added was the city of Brooklyn, as were Queens and Staten Island.

"Even if Staten Island was close to where we lived," Jimmy explained, "you had to take a streetcar an' then a ferry to get there. Pop puts on a suit an' tie. Mama wears a hat an' her best dress. They is all set to go when, suddenly, Pop runs back to the barbershop. A couple of minutes later he comes out draggin' his Victrola. It's so heavy, he's breathin' heavy. I ask him, 'Pop, what are you doin'?'

" 'Maybe they don't have no music in Staten Island,' he answers. 'What good is a vacation an' no music?' I finally talk him out of it, but he's real mad. *'Snomagogna'* he keeps yellin' over an' over. The first words Pop used when he came to America were: snom—*agogna*—son of a gun, *mangiare*—eat, and *costa troppa*—costs too much."

Years later gossip columnist Hedda Hopper wrote a story about Jimmy's success. In it she mentioned the Victrola incident and referred to Bartolomeo as "Bizarre Bart." He was so pleased with his nickname that he made Lillian order some calling cards:

BIZARRE BART
Father of the Famous Jimmy Durante
Good Haircuts and Shaves

When New York City's Mayor Fiorello LaGuardia declared an official "Shnozzola Day" (May 8, 1939), Bartolomeo sat beside his son in an open car and majestically handed out the cards. Although he took great pride in his son's success, he refused to watch him perform. "Show business is *impuro*," he said. Bartolomeo was eighty-one years old when he first saw Jimmy's act.

"Well, Pop," Schnozzola asked. "How did you like it?"

"Lissen, son," his father replied. "Les not get in a argument."

"But the truth is that Papa was disappointed when Jimmy didn't stick to classical music," Lillian said. "When Jimmy was about eleven years we got a piano for him to play. He'd sit there and practice all the time. But what came out was never the kind of music Papa liked. The piano was given to us by one of our cousins who didn't have room for it. Lord, it was huge—we had to get it in through the window. Naturally, Papa directed the moving. The walls were all scarred and the glass in the window was smashed."

In exchange for the piano, Bartolomeo agreed to give his relative free haircuts for the rest of his life. Professor Angelo Fiori, a local music teacher, was engaged for fifty cents a lesson. The professor, who had a big, black mustache and chin whiskers, was madly in love with a British nanny who worked in Boston. Since he spoke little English, lessons were mainly devoted to Jimmy writing elaborate, ungrammatical letters for his teacher. Fiori would dictate amorous passages.

Evidently, the letters were not very persuasive. After three of them, Fiori's sweetheart wrote that she never wanted to hear from him again. Jimmy had been afraid to read her rejection letter accurately. Instead, he said that she was forced to sever relations because her mother was dying of TB and wanted her back in England. Fiori learned differently when the letter was translated by a neighbor. To escape the wrath of the grieving music teacher, Jimmy tried to convince his parents that Fiori wasn't to be trusted. "He wants me to come twice a week so he can make more money out of us," Jimmy said. "He's a robber!"

Bartolomeo Durante's response was, *"Giacoma,* better learn good!" Jimmy continued to take lessons, but whenever he had a chance, he would sneak down to a saloon that was near his house. Eight Fingers Rogers, a New Orleans pianist was featured. "I'd stand there for hours listenin' to him play rag," Durante said. "It would send me into another world. Then I'd go home an' try to play in exactly the same way."

"Ragtime is more than mere music," said Charles Evans Hughes in 1916 when he campaigned unsuccessfully for the Presidency against Woodrow Wilson. "It is an evil way of life," Hughes added. "Ragtime makes youth rebel against all authority. It has no place in a decent society."

Publisher William Randolph Hearst agreed. "Satan music," he called it. "The titles alone give you an indication of what to expect: 'Sour Grapes Rag,' 'Smash-Up Rag,' 'Hit and Skedaddle Rag,' 'Lovin' Woman Rag,' 'Doll Rag,' 'Ragtime Insanity.' Listen to them and you will realize how decadent they are!"

A Hearst editorial condemning ragtime once resulted in a near riot. A San Francisco music store selling piano-player rolls was stormed by angry adult protesters. Police had to bodily remove them. Disapproving actions such as this one was generally ignored by the young. Ragtime was the earliest form of jazz to have a large teenage following. Originally the music of black dance halls and whorehouse pianists, it soon swept the nation and much of Europe. It made converts of many classical composers. Claude Debussy and Igor Stravinsky admitted they had been greatly influenced by ragtime and incorporated the style in their own music.

A pianist playing ragtime would hold a steady beat with his

left hand while offsetting it with a tricky, syncopated beat played with his right. Ragtime was inspired by the ragged-time "Cake Walk," a high stepping dance popular in post-Civil War black face minstrel shows. The music was often primitive. A mixture of white folk songs and black work songs.

"I lived for it," Jimmy said. "Somehow it got to me. I'd bang away at it for hours."

Several times a month he earned fifty or seventy-five cents an evening by banging a honky-tonk piano at neighborhood parties, club dances, and bar mitzvahs. Once, the music critic of the *Jewish Daily Forward* wrote: "Young Mr. Durante may not be of our faith, but last night his harmonics at Howard Fingleman's thirteenth year celebration was appreciated by all. Even if it was somewhat frenzied."

Jimmy dropped out of school in the seventh grade. At the time, it wasn't considered very unusual. Less than 15,000 of the 500,000 pupils enrolled in the city's elementary schools completed eight terms. "My mother hoped I would graduate," he said. "But she could plainly see that it wasn't such a good idea. I'd come home from school so unhappy that I'd keep losin' weight. For her that was the worst thing that could happen to any child. So she let me quit. But I could tell how much sadness it caused her. She had hoped that I'd become a doctor or at least a drug store owner."

In quick succession, Jimmy took a series of temporary jobs. He worked in a local funeral parlor washing cadavers. He was a coal wagon driver. As "Kid Salerno" he fought one prize fight—KO'd in the first round. For a brief time he was an errand boy for the American Banknote Company.

His brother, Michael, was also employed by the banknote firm until he became ill and lost his job. Jimmy, usually mild tempered, was furious. He complained to the manager. As a result, he, too, was fired. "Maybe I was too vitribolical," Jimmy said. "But I get sore when someone is pushed around, especially someone so close to me. It wasn't nice of them to fire Mikey when he gets sick."

A job that Jimmy enjoyed tremendously was also short lived. For several weekends he pinch-hit for the full-time pianist at the Lyceum, a local movie theater. "In those days they never heard of talking pictures yet," he said. "They used to have this guy playin' the piano while they showed silent films. The regular guy is laid up with somethin' bad, so I take his place. I play battlin' music when the hero is duelin' with a sword while he's hangin' upside down on a steep mountain. It changes to smoochin' stuff when he's alone with his girl. Then it becomes church music when they get married. The other movie is with a cowboy star—there was always a double feature. He rescues this girl from a sneaky guy who robs her of her ranch; he's the sheriff so I play chasin' music while he rides after the bad guy."

Jimmy's family came to hear him. "Everybody except my father," he said. "Pop stays home. Just before I left for the theater, he yells, 'Only boozers play that way!' But my mother is there an' she gets so excited, she keeps applauding me. She runs out when the owner walks up an' down the aisle with a flit-gun. The sweet smellin' stuff he sprays makes her sick at her stomach. But when I get home she says, '*Giacoma*, you not boozer. You do nice.'"

3

Diamond Tony's

Although Durante was never considered a "boozer," he admitted being captivated by a saloon's swinging doors. "There's somethin' romantic about them," he said. "Every time I'd push one open an' see a piano player playin', I'd start thinkin', 'If only I had a job like that, I'd be set for life.' "

In 1910, when he was seventeen years old, a neighbor who worked as a bartender in Diamond Tony's, a beer hall in Coney Island, told him about an opening for a pianist. Coney Island is an island in name only. Most of the area that once separated it from Brooklyn had long been filled in. At the turn of the century, its six mile beach was the gayest and toughest playground in the world. Summer crowds fought for a spot on the sand. Following a quick dip in the water it was customary to stroll along the boardwalk and visit freak shows, shooting galleries, and amusement parks. Riders were whirled, jostled, and tossed upside down. After sunset, the dimly lit cabarets that lined the side streets were filled with noisy revelers.

Jimmy's opinion of the beachfront resort wasn't very flattering. He and Marvin Berman had been there briefly—very briefly. They had pooled their savings for a day's outing of

16

rides, side shows, and hot dogs. Just as they were about to purchase tickets to the roller coaster at Steeplechase, they discovered that all their money had been stolen.

The previous summer Coney Island had been the scene of a sensational gangland triple slaying. Andrew Russo, Blanche Love, his current mistress, and his bodyguard, Salvatore Ippolito, were eating dinner in one of the local nightclubs. In the midst of the soup course they were gunned down. A waiter who had witnessed the murders identified the McBride twins, members of a competing mob, as the slayers. The McBrides claimed they were shooting dice with the boys when the hit occurred. The "boys" confirmed their alibi. Not that it would have mattered if they hadn't as Coney Island police were well known for being soft on crime.

Jimmy, fearful of his family's reaction, hadn't told them about the Coney Island job. However, they soon found out. Bartolomeo started swearing. Albert warned his brother about Coney Island, "I'm certain that the place is a hell hole. It's probably filled with gangsters and prostitutes. If you don't want to wind up as a pimp or something worse, don't go!"

"Al's right!" Michael Durante said. "No one in the entire family has ever sunk so low as being a saloon pianist. I've seen them with glasses of beer and whiskey on top of the piano, and a willing girl waiting for the number to end!"

"Gee, fellows, I promise I won't do any kind of funny business," Jimmy protested.

Albert started to reply when he was interrupted by Rosa who walked in carrying a small bundle. Carefully, she untied the parcel. Out fell a long shank of hair. It was her own that she had saved for years. She placed the hair on the sink counter and reached for a match. Her youngest son was startled. "Mama, what are you doing?" he asked.

"Can't you tell!" Albert said. "It's a custom from the old country. Mama wants to burn the hair so she can keep her son from going around with whores! She wants to save you!"

Jimmy put his arms around his mother. "Mama, you know I don't do any chasin'. I promise I won't even touch no girl. Please don't worry!"

The next morning he put on his cap and a black turtleneck sweater—standard uniform for saloon pianists—and took off for Coney Island. His nose had already reached full growth: length 2½ inches, elevation 3¼ inches. So had his physique: height 5 feet 7 inches, weight 135 pounds. He had large ears, tiny eyes, a recessive chin, and a declining hairline. Robert Benchley once described him as, "Possessing a face and body that anyone with 20/2200 vision could admire."

Albert had been right about the place. Beauty had no room there; any owner who spent money on drapes and decorations would have been read out of the local Chamber of Commerce. Customers didn't come to sit and look at pretty furniture. They wanted a good time and could get it with loud music, available girls, and plenty to drink. Many of them never even knew—or cared—that there was an ocean nearby.

Diamond Tony's was a large, gloomy looking beer hall on Oceanic Walk. It was surrounded by other third-rate cabarets. The pianist performed on a tiny, unpainted wooden platform that was encircled by several dozen tables, covered with badly stained red checkered oilcloths. A balcony stretched across the full length of the cavernous room. Bending over a low railing, with their bare bosoms protruding, were six heavily painted ladies. They were hookers who serviced clients in upstairs rooms. Singing waiters functioned as their procurers.

Whenever the waiter spotted a potential customer sitting at his station, he'd start singing, "Come down you beautiful babe, there's company waiting. So come on down!" The most successful pair was a waiter called Mad Pipes and his lady in harness, Ready Sadie. Each week, Tony awarded a bottle of Scotch to the twosome that produced the most business. Mad Pipes and Ready Sadie broke a house record when they came in first for fifteen consecutive weeks. To attract additional business, Diamond Tony allowed a patron to pick up a girl on the boardwalk. After buying a few drinks, he'd be permitted to take her upstairs. Of course there was a cover charge for the privilege.

Jimmy quickly learned why the boss was called Diamond Tony. All the buttons on his jacket were sparkling fake diamonds. He wore huge imitation diamond rings on his two pinky fingers. His greatest humiliation was when a thief robbed him of his wallet and pocket watch. Then in full hearing range of an employee, the holdup man said contemptuously, "You can keep those phony diamonds. My wife just bought better ones in a dollar store."

However, the thief's taunt didn't make Tony shed his ersatz gems. After brandishing them at Jimmy, he asked him to play "Maple Leaf Rag." "I suppose you're better than nothing," he said when the number was finished. "Okay, you start tonight. Fifteen dollars a week." Before Jimmy could thank him, he added, "You'll be on the second shift which means playing from seven until the place closes."

"I soon found out," said Jimmy. "He meant from seven to unconscious." The only chance the youngster had to take a break was when a song plugger from Tin Pan Alley came in and wanted to do his own playing. "It gave me some time to grab a sandwich," Jimmy said. "Otherwise, Tony would keep watchin' you closely. If you'd go to the gent's room, he'd yell, 'What are you tryin' to do? Take advantage?' When business was slow, Tony would stand in front of the place to lasso a passerby. Each time he'd see a likely prospect, he'd clap his hands to signal me. Then I'd start playin' as fast an' loud an' furious as I could."

Shortly after Durante was hired, Tony lured in a customer who was already quite drunk. The intoxicated man polished off a dozen additional beers, then he began smashing tables and chairs. The bouncer, a former heavyweight boxer, was ordered to toss him out. Instead, the customer threw out the bouncer. An emergency call was made to the police. But by the time the law made an appearance, he had loosened several of Tony's teeth and blackened both his eyes.

"It didn't teach Tony a lesson," said Jimmy. "A few weeks later he does exactly the same thing. This time it's a henpecked husband tryin' to dodge his wife. The lady tracks her husband to an upstairs room where he is in the middle of romancin' one of the girls. Before he even has time to put back on his pants, his wife drags him outside. There were lots of things like that. Not only did I get a chance to improve my piano playin', but I became a walkin' encyclopedic of human nature. I learned you never jump to concussions—that there's always a good reason for how people act. I also found out that most of the girls didn't work there because they like it."

Undoubtedly, the prostitutes in Diamond Tony's were kind to Jimmy because he treated them with respect. "Sure, I knew they was fallin' ladies," he said. "But still they was females. An' to me that's sacred." Although most of them were near his own age, they acted motherly toward Durante. They would gather around the piano and compliment his playing, caution him to watch his diet, and invariably tweak his nose for good luck. One of them went to Hollywood where she achieved some moderate success as a film actress.

"I never told a livin' soul about the line of work she used to be in," Durante said. "But one of them fan magazines finds out an' prints it. On the day the story comes out, that upset girl calls me up on the telephone. I expect her to start swearin' at me, so before she could start, I tell her that it never came from my lips. 'I didn't think that for a minute,' she says. 'I knew you wouldn't do a thing like that. The rat who squealed was an old boyfriend.' Soon we're both cryin. That poor girl was a good kid who just had a lot of bad breaks."

The incident occurred when the movie industry was passing through one of its periodic endorsements of morality. Her contract wasn't renewed. She returned to New York where she resumed her former career. Several years later she told a reporter, "Schnozzola was the only decent person in Diamond Tony's. He almost restored my faith in men, even if he kept refusing the freebies I offered him."

Jimmy's special friend was a twenty-year-old brunette named Gladie. "She was real beautiful," he said. "I had promised my family I wouldn't do no chasin', but I got to admit a strong feelin' for Gladie. So when she asks me if she could borrow my ring for a night so she could impress her landlady, with pleasure I hand it to her."

His mother had given him the ring on his sixteenth birthday. "It belonged to her grandmother," he said. "She tells me that her grandmother gave it to her before she left for America. 'So take good care of it, *Giacoma*. It's worth more than a hundred dollars.' Gladie don't come back the next night. I become nervous when she don't show up the next night either. It was the same way for two more weeks. I'd watch for her, but no Gladie. Then, suddenly, she comes in. She tells me she hocked the ring to pay for a certain kind of ladies' operation but promises to get it back. Then she is gone again. I try to find her, but she disappears from the face of the earth. Finally I tell my mother that I lost the ring."

Years later, Durante was a headliner at a nightclub, when he was approached by a cadaverous looking old lady. "Jimmy," she said, kissing his cheek. "How are your parents?"

"My mother passed away," Jimmy said looking puzzled.

"Don't you recognize me?" she said.

"Yeah, sure. You're from the old neighborhood."

"No, that's not it. I'm Gladie. I always could tell you'd go far."*

---

* Gladie died of an advanced case of malnutrition in New York's Bellevue Hospital in 1958. Her possessions were stored in a paper bag: torn lingerie, a crucifix, a map of Florida, and a thick bundle of Durante's clippings. She had listed him as next of kin. When he was notified, he paid for the funeral.

4

Enter Eddie Cantor

Toward the end of September 1911, business slackened off at Diamond Tony's and Jimmy was let go. He soon found another piano playing job at the Chatham Club in New York's Chinatown. The Chatham was a notorious hangout for gangsters. Durante knew many of them from his neighborhood. Although he himself wasn't a criminal he realized they were all around. He'd shake his head sadly and look the other way. His attitude toward them had been formed when he was a youngster.

"There are lots of reasons for my feelin's," he said. "From the time I started walkin' I knew all about the Black Hand an' the Mafia. I saw a lot of good they did—everybody who ever lived on the Lower East Side has to feel like me. There was this lady across the street from us who had a bunch of unlucky things happen to her. First, her daughter gets run over by a trolley car an' is crippled for life. Then the lady's husband gets sick with the big C an' dies from it. If that ain't enough, her only son, just a young kid, is tryin' to make some extra dough by paintin' a house. So what happens? He falls off the ladder an' also gets crippled. She can't pay her rent, an' the landlord wants to kick her out with the crippled son an' crippled daughter. That's when the Mafia marches in. Not only do they make the landlord change his mind, but give the lady each month some regular money to live on. I could tell you plenty of other stories like that one. Sure, I know those men do lots of terrible things, but it's hard for me to hate someone from what I see with my own eyes."

Jimmy spoke well of most people. He excepted patrons of the Chatham Club. "The characters in that place were positively looney," he said. "I overhear one customer talking on the telephone to his girlfriend. He's askin' her for a date for that evenin'. I guess she tells him 'no' because he becomes historical an' starts screamin'. 'If you don't see me for a date tonight,' he yells, 'I swear I'll blow my brains out!' Then he pulls out a revolver, an' so help me, he points it straight at his head an' pulls the trigger. Lucky, he ain't such a good shot. He blows his toe off. It was that kind of place."

Jimmy felt the only good thing about the Chatham Club was its location. "It was just a few blocks away from where I lived," Durante said. "I was able to get there in less than a few minutes tops, so I was never late except that one time." Before I could ask him about that one time, he blurted out, "It was when my cousin, Teresa, God rest her soul, burned to death."

Jimmy attended the funeral and then visited with her mother, Bartolomeo's younger sister. Fifteen-year-old Teresa was a seamstress who perished in a fire. She worked for Triangle Shirtwaist Company, which was notorious for its sweatshop conditions. It occupied the top three floors of a ten-story building that was near Washington Square. Late Saturday afternoon on March 25, 1911, 600 girls, most of them Italian and Jewish immigrants between the ages of thirteen and twenty-three years old, were at their sewing machines. At 5 P.M., just as the bell sounded quitting time, fire broke out on the 8th floor. Seconds later, the ninth and tenth floors were blazing. Unable to escape, more than 125 girls died. Most were burned to death; some attempted to jump out of windows—the street was littered with mangled bodies.

There was startling evidence that exits had been purposely

locked to prevent unauthorized trips to the bathroom. The Triangle owners were charged with manslaughter, but were acquitted. Hearing the verdict, enraged courtroom spectators started stamping their feet and shouting, "Guilty murderers! Guilty murderers!"

As a result of the tragedy, a New York state factory-study committee was formed.* Members recommended a new safety code that was the strongest in the nation. Labor unions, then ignored, began using the Triangle fire as a rallying cry.

"The priest who was at the funeral service thought Teresa's death had a good reason," Jimmy said. "Me, I just don't know. The day of the funeral, I come to work at the Chatham maybe an hour after I was supposed to. The boss acts like I'm a month late. 'Do that again,' he yells, 'an' I'll have one of my boys part your hair with a club!' I don't think he's kiddin', but to tell the truth, I don't care what he says. All I could think about was poor Teresa." The grief was still very evident as he recalled the tragic incident. "What makes a person do such terrible things?" he asked. "Is it because they're more interested in makin' money then in anythin' else?"

It was obvious that he didn't want a reply, and answered his own question. "Mr. Stires, who owned the Chatham, was like that," he said. "It didn't matter that his place was dead as a doornail until past midnight when the regulars start driftin' in. He still made me come in by seven o'clock an' stay until five or six the next mornin'." Late hours ruled at the Chatham. "That place was a mint," Jimmy said. "The cash register smoked from ringin' up numbers. But I learned, you can't make customers act as if they're in church. They were out for a good time, an' figure they couldn't have it without lots of noise, booze, an' plenty of brawls."

There were so many drunken fist fights and shootings in the Chatham Club that the police were forced to do something about it. They ordered it to close at 1:00 A.M. "That was like

---

* Frances Perkins was a very aggressive member of the committee. Years later she became President Franklin D. Roosevelt's Secretary of Labor. She was the first woman Cabinet member in U.S. history.

hangin' crepe on the door," Jimmy said. "For two or three days we just sit around doin' nothin' while the trade is goin' elsewhere. After a week of this, the boss gets boilin' mad. 'I pay those police plenty,' he yells. 'But they don't want to listen. If anybody is goin' to ruin this joint, I'll do it myself!' He picks up a chair an' throws it at the chandelier. Then he tosses a seltzer bottle at a mirror, breaks all the glasses behind the bar. Those that ain't broken, he pegs through the big plate glass window. I never met anyone since as hard-boiled as Mr. Stires. I'll say this for him—it took nerve to do what he did!"

That summer Jimmy returned to Coney Island. This time his piano playing was at Carey Walsh's, a cabaret several doors from Diamond Tony's. "It was a little fancier," he recalled. "The bouncer wore a soup-an'-fish suit an' there was a sign in the toilet that says GENTS, PLEASE BUTTON-UP YOUR FLY. One of the singin' waiters was a skinny, little guy with big, black eyes, whose name was Eddie Cantor. Me an' him hit it right off an' became good friends."

Durante would become ecstatic when he talked about Cantor. "That Eddie was tops," he'd say. "We seemed to match. If a customer asks for a song, an' we didn't know it, we made one up on the spot. For example, if the guy wanted sometin's called "Springtime In Kalamazoo," which Eddie an' me never heard of, I'd fake the melody an' Eddie would sing, 'Oh, it's springtime in Ol' Kalamazoo-oo . . .' Then he'd turn away an' do some double-talk singin'. Most of the time the guy who asked for the special song would be so drunk, he wouldn't notice. But sometimes, he'd get nasty an' complain, 'That's not the one I asked for!' Eddie would be ready for him. 'Oh, you mean this one,' he'd say. Then he'd make up some other lyrics: 'I always feel so blue thinking about you, when it's springtime in Kalamazoo . . .' I'd follow along on the piano. 'No!' the customer would say again. 'That's not it either. I'm going to report both of you to your boss!' "

"That would be Jimmy's cue to step in," Cantor once told journalist Quentin Reynolds. "With a straight face, Schnozzola would say something soothing like, 'Hey, fellow, you sure are the smart one to be able to spot those wrong songs.

You must be some kind of a musical genius!' Most of the time, that customer would be so flattered, that instead of reporting us, he'd leave a generous tip ... Schnozz was comical in everything he did."

Cantor spoke of Carey Walsh giving Jimmy an assignment to be on the lookout for customers who tried to sneak out before paying the check. " 'Don't worry about a thing,' Jimmy told his boss. 'This nose I got can smell out a chisler from a mile away.' The way he went about it was a mad riot. Whenever he noticed a deadbeat, he'd practically slide off the piano stool while furiously playing a prearranged disaster song. It was a signal. Then, Jimmy would play dirge tunes as he watched the bouncer tackle the customer before he got through the door."

Since Cantor also lived on the Lower East Side, he and Jimmy would frequently go to work together. They'd arrive early so they might earn some extra money working as shills at a boardwalk shooting gallery. The owner made use of their innocent looking appearance. Bells would start ringing as Cantor clumsily fired his gun. "A perfect bull's eye!" the gallery owner would shout. "And from a man who never before held a gun in his hand! So step right up!"

While selecting a prize, Cantor would stage-whisper, "Jimmy, that was real easy. Now, it's your turn!" Durante would awkwardly lift up a rifle. The same thing happened when he fired: a bull's-eye.

"What did I tell you?" shouted the gallery owner. "Another amateur wins!" After their victories, Eddie and Jimmy would go to the rear of the gallery, where they'd exchange their prizes for cash. Usually, they'd spend some of the money on frankfurters at Feltman's Fast-Food Restaurant. When Feltman raised the price of a frank from a nickel to a dime, they advised Nathan Handwerker, a Feltman employee, to open a rival hot dog stand and return to the five cent price. He did.*

A pretty, red haired teenager helped Nathan with the serving in his new stand. She didn't do it for very long. Several months later, a Hollywood talent scout with a passion for hot

---

*Nathan's developed into a multi-million dollar business.

dogs saw her. He made her lipstick her mouth in the shape of a Cupid's bow, rouge her cheeks as well as her knees, put on a short skirt that gave a glimpse of the tops of her rolled silk stockings and wear her hair short with marcelled stiff waves. Renamed Clara Bow she soon became the flapper "It" girl movie star of the Roaring Twenties.

While still employed at Nathan's, she brought Cantor and Durante packages of free frankfurters. They were gifts from her grateful boss who wished to express his appreciation. Before Jimmy and Eddie had a chance to take their booty home, Bedbug Bertha, a local vagrant that Walsh allowed to panhandle inside the cabaret—rumor had it that she was his mother—smelled the two packages. Greedily, she tore them open and quickly devoured the contents.

"So what if I didn't get to eat those free franks," Jimmy said philosophically. "If I never worked at Carey Walsh's, it figures I might never have met Eddie Cantor. In a way he changed my whole life." Cantor was partly responsible for Durante becoming a professional comedian. During the time they worked together, he'd constantly tell him that piano playing in dives could only lead to a dead end.

"What else can I do?" Jimmy would ask.

"Everybody likes you. Get out on the floor and tell jokes."

"Gee, Eddie, I couldn't do that. I'd be afraid they'd start laughing."

Razor Riley, Pretty Boy Moran, Etc.

By the time Jimmy was twenty-one years old, he had played ragtime piano in more than a dozen cabarets. "I was gettin' used to them," he said. 'An' they all started lookin' alike—a bar, a piano, tables, girls, an' singin' waiters. Then in 1914 I start to work in Brooklyn, at a place called Maxine's on Rockwell Place and Fulton Street. I soon find out it has all those things, but somethin' more. It is filled with the oddest an' toughest characters I ever met. Even more weird then those at the Chatham Club. Here, if you took off your hat, they thought you was a sissy!"

Razor Riley was one of Maxine's star customers. He had earned his name by carving up rival gangsters with a large bowie knife he always carried in a specially crafted red leather pouch. "Those stiffs look like confetti when I finish with them," he boasted.

"For some reason, Razor took a likin' to me," Jimmy said. "He invites me to a party in Valley Stream in Long Island. I don't feel like goin' to a party, but I don't want to argue with his knife. So I get in the car. We go only a few miles when I learn the party is Razor's way of sayin' he's about to polish off some guy he calls Hurry-Up Harry an' dump his sliced up body on a deserted road. We drive to Hurry-Up's house, but he ain't there. Then we visit a couple of bars he's supposed to go to. Again, no dice. But at each place, Razor says to the bartender, 'Be sure to tell Hurry-Up that Ragtime Jimmy is lookin' for him!' Suddenly, I realize that when the dead body is found, I'll get the blame. I breathe a sigh of relief when the hit is called off because they make up and pull a job together."

Another story that Jimmy enjoyed telling concerned Pretty Boy Moran, who was also a Maxine's regular when he wasn't in prison. Pretty Boy was extremely fond of his luxuriant waxed mustache. He had once been told that it made him look like a movie actor. Ever since it had become his most prized possession. He went into hiding after he wounded a bank guard in an attempted robbery. Government authorities distributed thousands of wanted posters containing his picture. However, it was an old photograph and showed him clean shaven. He was caught in a Dayton, Ohio, post office penciling in the missing mustache.

Late in 1915, police closed Maxine's for disorderly conduct —four separate homicides had occurred there in one week! Again, Jimmy was unemployed. But knowledge of his piano playing ability had spread. Sam Sakerton, proprietor of the Alamo, a nightclub on Harlem's 125th Street, offered him a job. The salary was eighty-five dollars a week—thirty dollars more than he had been earning at Maxine's. In addition to pounding out ragtime, he was put in charge of booking entertainment and starting a five-piece band.

Jimmy would proudly jump up from the piano to lead the band. "It was my first big billin'," he said. "An' I wanted everybody to know about it. I also had to hire dancers, singers an' specialty acts. More then a few turned out to be real lushes. One was a girl singer. When she's sober enough to walk, she sings like an angel. But when she's drinkin', she can't even remember the words. So I tell her I have to let her go. When I do, she polishes off a quart of booze in record time. In front of the whole place she claims she's Lady Godivin' an' takes off every stitch of clothes.

"If that ain't enough, there was this guy who gives impressions of famous celebrities. The trouble is that he has sticky fingers an' the silverware ain't safe. When he'd get good an' drunk, he'd even steal the glasses. Once he steals a glass with the drink still in it. He puts it in his pocket when no one is lookin'. Right in the middle of his imitation of Theodore Roosevelt, it comes pourin' out.

"But thank God not all of them were like that. There was a lady dancer who had a lot of personality—the way she danced was nobody's business. One night this Englishman drops by an' sees her. He keeps comin' back. Eventually, the lady disappears from the scene. I hear she marries this Englishman who turns out to be the owner of a hotel in London where she is now livin' in luxury. The other girls all hoped that someone like that would happen to them. But the sad truth is that there were lots more crooks an' hoods then millionaire hotel keepers."

Big Joe Tennyson was one of the hoods. He liked the way Jimmy played "Meadowbrook Fox Trot," and would tip him generously. The sum would increase whenever Tennyson was successful at his work. Big Joe was a burglar. "Even though I know Mr. Tennyson is a stickup man," said Jimmy, "he is always polite to his wife, a nice looking, skinny lady. They'd always come in holdin' hands like Romeo an' Julius. He is overjoyed when his wife gives birth to a baby girl. Everyone in the Alamo is invited to party after the baby's Christenin'. I bring the whole band. When the janitor complains about the noise, Big Joe breaks three of his ribs. Also the lease."

One night, three masked men entered the Alamo brandishing guns. The trio's leader mounted the band stand. "No one will get hurt if you do as we say!" he shouted. Jimmy recognized the voice—it belonged to Big Joe Tennyson.

"I don't let on," Durante said. "But I'm fearin' for Mr. Sakerton's bum ticker, so I tell him the boss has a leaky pump an' to take it easy with him. Instead of listenin', he says, 'Get back to the piano, big nose!' I don't want to argue with him.

'Yes, sir,' I say real quick. 'Would you like me to play somethin' special?' That makes him real mad. 'Start playin',' he says, 'or you'll get somethin' special between your eyes!' "

The masked men relieved the customers and the staff of money and jewelry. "They take thirty-two dollars from me," Jimmy said. "Twenty of it had been a tip from a rich butter an' egg man that liked my playin'. I was thinkin' of how I'd spend it when those masked guys came in. Before they leave, Big Joe comes over to me and wants to know if I recognized him. 'I never saw you before in my life,' I lie. 'That's good, pal,' he says. 'Sorry I pushed you around, but you got to learn not to get out of line. When you listen, you're not so bad. I'll be around to hear you play.' He says it real nice. I tell him, 'Please do. An' be sure to bring the missus.' "

As soon as the gunmen left, Jimmy was asked by Sakerton what the conversation had been all about. "He just wanted to apologize," Jimmy replied. "He told me that he'll be back."

"Oh, my God!" Sakerton said clutching his chest. "Not again?"

"Only socially," Jimmy assured him.

That wasn't Durante's first experience with being robbed. Just three weeks before, a girl telephoned him to meet her at 123 West 101st Street when he got through work. "I go there at five o'clock in the mornin'," Jimmy said. "I find the address is an empty lot. A hansom cab drives up an' two men get out. They pull me in, rip off my socks an' drape them over the horse's ears, take my pants, an' throw me out almost naked at the corner of 116th Street an' Eighth Avenue. I manage to get back to the Alamo. Sakerton is still there. Here I am freezin' an' he tells me he plans to open up a branch in Coney Island. He asks me for a good name. So with practically nothin' on I tell him to call the place 'The Ice Box Arms.' But it's called 'The College Arms.' Like the Alamo it also was pretty wild, but it did have a classy name. Soon Sakerton buys another Coney Island cabaret that we call 'The College Inn.' He makes me a rovin' manager."

Visitors to those clubs were resigned to being cheated. A crooked taxi driver would tell his out-of-town passengers about a place where they could have a good time. Men who should have known better accepted the invitation. They would start drinking with the hostesses who worked on a percentage of the take. Their job was to make you buy "imported" champagne. When the customer was quite drunk, he'd be presented with the bill. Usually, it was three or four times higher than was actually spent. Even if the whopping padding was noticed, it did little good to protest. The bouncer—always mountain sized—suddenly made an appearance.

If the customer didn't have sufficient cash, the obliging cashier would agree to take a check. After it was written, he would carefully examine the signature, shake his head, and sadly announce that it was illegible. Then he'd pretend to tear it up. The inebriated customer would promptly write another. When he arrived home, he'd discover that both checks had been cashed.

"But the next time that guy comes to town," Jimmy prophesied. "He'll do exactly the same thing. So long as the girls keep smilin', the piano player keeps playin', an' the corks go poppin', the sucker will always come back!"

6

The High-Hat Cakewalker

"Havin' true-blue friends is the strongest thing a person can have goin' for them in the whole world," Jimmy said. "An' I'm blessed with a lot. That's why to them I always give the big hello. But to the fewer closer-ups who are my intermate friends an' have no exterior motives to grind, I give my special big hello only to them."

Yes, it is an involved statement. However, like most of Schnozzola's complicated sentences, his facial expressions and body movements helped one to decipher them. His face would actually glow when he talked about his "intermate" friends. One of the "closer-ups" was Eddie Jackson, who always wore a black top hat when performing his specialty—the cakewalk.* In 1915, he entered Jimmy's life, and remained there for sixty-five years. "Eddie is one of my very best all-time pals," Durante said. "Me an' him went through a lot of thick an' thins."

Three years younger than Durante, Jackson was born in

*In the late 1880s the cakewalk was an elaborate way of strolling. It was performed mainly by Southern blacks. A cake was awarded to the person executing the fanciest steps. About a dozen years later it developed into a strutting dance.

Brooklyn to Jewish parents. The family name was Jacobs. Eddie's mother hoped that he'd become a rabbi like her grandfather and three uncles. Instead, after completing elementary school, he tried to get a booking as a nightclub singer. Told that he was too young, he took a job as an apprentice machine operator in a bookbindery where his foreman was Al Capone, the future gangster chief.

"I'd always sing while I was working," Jackson said. "Al would always applaud. I think that is what helped me decide to try show business again." At the time, Capone appeared to be a law-abiding citizen, but even then his crime-organizing ability was evident. He'd be told to turn out a thousand books. Capone would instruct his crew to give him several hundred more. Then he'd sell the surplus volumes at bargain prices. He'd reward his obliging staff with silk shirts and free copies of the pirated books. Since many were about English history, Jackson had a unique knowledge of Queen Victoria, Buckingham Palace, and the House of Lords. Plus a large wardrobe of striped silk shirts.

"Maybe if Jimmy had worked there instead of me, Al would have followed the straight and narrow," Jackson told Sime Silverman, founder of *Variety*, the show business bible. "His goodness rubs off on everybody he gets near." Jackson idolized Durante so much that he tried desperately to become his clone, even adopting his ailments. When Jimmy was told that he had been deferred from military duty in World War I because of a slight heart murmur and flat feet, Eddie said that he too was similarly afflicted.

"It didn't do no good that doctors told him he was in tip-top shape," Durante said. "He'd claim they were lyin' an' he was really on a death door. I know Eddie's a hippochondrian, but it's not right for a person to stop lovin' someone because of somethin' they can't stop doin'. Still the same, I wish he wouldn't keep tellin' everyone that he has a lot more education than me!"

Jackson's academic boast was the result of his completing elementary school—eighth grade—whereas Durante left in the seventh grade. However, one of Eddie's brothers revealed the reason for the diploma. "Eddie kept being left back," he said. "The principal decided the only way to get rid of him was by letting him graduate. He figured that Eddie wasn't such a good influence on the other kids."*

Eddie Jackson was the czar of the school's number racket. For a nickel investment, a student in Public School 55 could win a shiny silver dollar if he correctly guessed the number of pieces of broken chalk there were in a jar Eddie kept in the janitor's broom closet. He was constantly inventing chancy schemes. Underneath Jackson's graduation picture in the school yearbook was the prediction: "Eddie will be a Wall Street millionaire by the time he's twenty-one."

Jackson didn't become a financial magnate, but occasionally he did earn as much as $300 a week from his unique style of dancing and singing. Late in 1915, Jimmy hired Eddie and his partner, Dot Taylor, to entertain at the Alamo. Their strong point was the then popular shimmy dance. When the audience failed to appreciate the act, Taylor decided to go elsewhere and try it with someone else. By then, Durante and Jackson had become close friends. Eddie was kept on as a singing waiter.

He specialized in singing war ballads. Few armed conflicts inspired such deep felt melodies as those composed during World War I: "Keep the Home Fires Burning," "Over There," "Pack Up Your Troubles," "Till We Meet Again," "There's A Long, Long Trail," "We Are Coming in Yankee Doodle Style." Each night, Durante would play a medley of the patriotic songs while Jackson crooned them. More songs were written then than at any other time. During the twenties, a billion copies of popular sheet music were sold each year at fifty cents apiece.

"The crowd would go wild when Jackson sang," Jimmy said. "I'll bet there wasn't a dry eye in the place when he'd finish. Sometimes he'd be joined by another singin' waiter, Harry Harris, who was once in the army. He still had his uniform and he'd put it on for those songs. One night they're

*Author Gene Fowler said that Jackson was allowed to graduate only after agreeing to a deal made by the principal: Eddie would receive his diploma if he learned to recite "Casey's Revenge," a sequel to "Casey at the Bat."

in the middle of 'Over There,' when Eddie shoves a hunk of pie in a customer's face. This guy was talkin' loud while they're singin'. He won't stop an' becomes even more noisy. So Eddie walks over to his table, reaches for the pie the guy is eatin', an' plop! Boy, it was slick. Buster Keaton could take lessons."

Jackson expected to be fired because of the incident. "I sure thought I'd get the gate," he said. "But Jimmy went to bat for me. Somehow, he convinced Sakerton to keep me on. He was forever doing things like that for me. The Alamo didn't have a microphone. Jimmy showed me how to sing loud without one. He'd pick out the songs for me. From experience, he knew the ones that would go over best. He had this fantastic feeling for the rhythms, a genius for tempo—not too fast, or too slow."

Durante also taught Jackson how to coax money out of people by singing songs they liked. "Throwin' money has gone out of fashion," Jimmy said. "Nowadays, an entertainer makin' only coffee an' cake money wouldn't lower himself to pick it up. But in the old days me an' Eddie Jackson depended on it. We worked hard to pull it out of customers' pockets. 'My Gal Sal' was the best coaxer. Other songs that made people want to give were: 'Will You Love Me in December As You Do in May?,' 'I Wish I Had My Old Gal Back,' and 'All Aboard to Blanket Bay.' The worst were: 'The Big, Big Storm,' 'Nobody Wants Me,' and 'You May Think I'm A Monkey's Uncle, but I'm Not Even Anyone's Cousin.'"

One night, Al Capone, who was rapidly becoming kingpin of the Chicago underworld, walked into the Alamo wearing a striped yellow suit and a pair of matching spats. He was closely guarded by two of his henchmen. They started making obscene cracks about Jimmy's nose. Jackson approached his former boss and whispered in his ear. Capone turned to the offenders. "This is my friend, Eddie Jackson," he said. "He's okay. And any friend of his has to be okay, also. So stop your kidding around! *Capisce?*"

After the club closed, Capone insisted on driving Jimmy and Eddie home. They shared a room in a Brooklyn boarding house. As they stepped out of the big, black armored Cadillac, the mobster handed each of them a hundred dollar bill. "That's a little something for your entertaining," he said. "And if you guys ever get to Chicago, be sure to look me up. I promise you'll have a good time." Then he drove away, followed by a smaller car filled with henchmen carrying machine guns.

"So what if those bills turned out to be counterfeit?" Jimmy said. "I'm only kiddin'—they were genuine green stuff. But that's not why I remember that night. It was because that was when I got the name Schnozzola. Jack Duffy of the vaudeville team of Bernard and Duffy gave it to me. He comes into the Alamo when Capone's boys are hecklin' me about my nose. I ask him to do a number. 'Sure, Schnozzola,' he says. Before that I had been known as Ragtime Jimmy. Now, I'll never be anythin' but Schnozzola. Them's the sad facts of life."

7

Schnozzola Takes a Wife

In addition to providing him with Eddie Jackson, a "boom" companion, the Alamo was also responsible for bringing Jeanne Olson into Jimmy's life. For twenty-two years, this badly matched couple shared a close, but too often destructive, marriage. Yet, during all that time, he rarely made a derogatory remark about the unfortunate union. The nearest he ever came was when he told Sime Silverman, the *Variety* editor, "Jeannie was one of the sweetest gals in the world when she wasn't sick. But now I know a person can be sick without all the time havin' to be in bed. The biggest mistake I ever made was to tell her she had to stay home to take care of the house. She never got over it. I keep askin' myself why I killed off talent like Jeannie, as things turned out."

They met in the winter of 1918, when she mistakenly came into the Alamo seeking a singing job. Her agent had sent her to a cabaret around the corner but she got lost. "In lots of ways, Jeannie was still a hick from the midwest," Jimmy said. "She was nothin' like where I came from."

Maude Jeanne Olson was born in Toledo, Ohio. When she was ten years old, her parents were divorced. She was sent to Detroit to live with her grandmother, who encouraged the youngster to cultivate her pleasant soprano voice, which she did by singing in the church choir and in a local vaudeville house. Her stage name was Maudie Jeanne. For the next dozen years she branched out and found employment in a series of midwestern theaters. In one of them, she was on the same bill as Lawrence Tibbett. "Young lady, your voice is very good," she claimed the famous opera star told her. She never forgot it and often quoted it to people she had just met.

"She must have told it to me more than a dozen times," Eddie Jackson said. "Just imagine how often she repeated it to Jimmy? Once, I was kidding and told her that it should be engraved on her tombstone. Was she mad. Wouldn't speak to me for months!"*

A few days after World War I started, Maudie Jeanne decided that her career wasn't progressing fast enough. She bought a one-way ticket to New York City. She was then twenty-six years old. Although she hadn't been expected at the Alamo, Durante agreed to give her an audition. When he accompanied her on the piano, she asked, "Whoever told you that you could play?"

"She told me that in such a cute way that I didn't even get mad," said Jimmy. "Instead, I start to laugh. An' so does she. Soon we're goin' out to get a bite to eat since the food in the Alamo gives you indigestion. By the end of the week we're makin' it a regular thing. I call her 'toots' an' she calls me 'tootis.' Then I start takin' her home to the room she lives in. I don't try no funny business. But after awhile when I want to kiss her she asks me, 'What are you, some kind of two-timer to your regular girlfriend?' "

Cuddles LeMay was the reason for Jeanne's skepticism. Cuddles, a striptease artist at a nearby burlesque house, thought Jimmy "too cunning for words." In between performances, she'd frequent the Alamo and shout, "Whoopee!" when he played the piano.

---

*Years later, Tibbett said, "Mrs. Durante must have misunderstood me. What I probably told her was that her voice wasn't half bad. I frequently complimented aspiring female vocalists in that manner. It was a harmless remark and it did make them ever so happy."

"It was plain that she likes me," Jimmy said. "I'm just a normal human person an' enjoy it. That makes Jeannie mad. I try to tell her that Cuddles don't mean nothin' to me, an' that I like her lots better than Cuddles." The situation was further complicated by an Alamo customer who was carried away by Jeanne's singing. To show his appreciation, he presented her with a bouquet of flowers and a large box of candy. These gifts came to Durante's attention.

"It turned me into a sourpuss overnight because I was so jealous," he said. "I really liked that girl, but she won't believe me. It takes Eddie Jackson to pull us back together. He tells her that I'm so unhappy that I want to commit suicide. God forbid. It's a little white lie, but it works."

Soon, however, Jackson was sorry that he had interceded. He was angry over one of Jimmy's practical jokes. "I didn't mean him no harm," Durante said innocently. "It happens when me an' Eddie an' Harry Harris are eatin' in a restaurant. Good naturedly, I whisper to Eddie that I'm goin' out with Jeannie that night an' don't want anybody to know about it except him.

" 'Wave your hand when I get to the cashier's desk,' I say in his ear.' Harry always kids me about my romancin' Jeannie. So that way he'll think I'm goin' home alone, but she'll meet me outside on the sly. Then I walk up to the cashier an' tell her that the fellow that's goin' to wave his hand is a signal that he's goin' to pay the check. Eddie waves his hand like we arrange an' I walk out free an' easy. After that, Eddie never waved his hand no more. Not even when he wants to go to the bathroom."

"You can't stay sore at Jimmy for very long," said Jackson. "There's something about that man that makes you want to keep him as a friend. A day later I was borrowing a pair of socks from him. He never intentionally wanted to hurt anybody's feelings. I sometimes think that was the reason why he married Jeanne. His mother was always telling him he should find himself a wife. To please her he got married, I was best man at the wedding. Just to be sociable I said to Jeanne that she made an attractive bride. That did it!

" 'When people have nothing better to say about a woman,'

she said bitterly, 'they call her attractive. For your information, I'm a healthy 5 foot 4 inch Nordic looking blonde with a charming upturned nose!' The way she said it made me shut up fast!"

Jimmy Durante and Jeanne Olson were wed on June 19, 1921, in Manhattan's St. Malachy's Catholic Church on West Forty-ninth Street. The wedding party consisted of relatives, friends, Alamo waiters, musicians, and customers. They accompanied the newlyweds to a picnic at Staten Island's South Beach. Bartolomeo asked his new daughter-in-law, "You be nice to my *Giacoma?*" When she nodded, he kissed her and added loudly, "*Giacoma* got himself a good wife."

Soon after the last guest left, the couple took a taxi to their first home, a small furnished room in a boarding house on Manhattan's Twenty-third Street. "That place was filled with cockroaches an' looked out on some kind of a shaft, but I didn't much care," Jimmy said. "It felt good to be goin' there with someone who just took my name."

The following day he reported for work alone. His startled spouse had just learned the reason. "I figure twenty-four hours a day bein' together spoils a marriage," he told her. "I'll get on your nerves an' you'll get on my nerves. So you have to quit your job an' stay home!"*

To replace Jeanne, he hired Big Tess Cardella. "Big Tess had a swell set of pipes," Durante said. "She was a big, hefty lady who weighed at least 300 pounds. One night, Big Tess decides to pull a Helen Morgan an' sing a song while she's sittin' on top of the piano. It caves in. We want to give it to the Salvation Army but they wouldn't take it because it's split so bad. Sam Sakerton said it was a lot cheaper when Jeannie did the singin'. But I wouldn't let her come back to work."

The Durantes planned to celebrate their first month anniversary by dining out at Rector's, a restaurant famous for its oyster stew and high society clientele. Instead, they had a bitter quarrel. Jimmy had promised to spend only a few

---

*Eddie Jackson's wife once opened a hat store on her own. Jimmy was very disturbed. He told him, "Your marriage is sure headed for the rocks when you let the wife wear the pants."

hours at the Alamo. "I'll definitely be home by 6:00 P.M.," he told Jeanne. When he walked in at 5:00 A.M., he was greeted by a very angry wife. That night, Jimmy slept on a cot that he set up in the kitchen.

Since the Durantes lived in a furnished room with kitchen privileges the other boarders were aware of the fight. "When one of them comes in to cook her breakfast," Jimmy said, "I sneak back to my room. Jeannie is still mad, but she finally starts laughin' when I tell her that maybe the kitchen is the right place for me, because that's where I first came into this world."

Eddie Jackson felt that Jeanne was constantly angry. "Jimmy wouldn't talk much about it," he said. "But I could tell by the way he acted. She objected to her husband being taken advantage of, his not getting a proper raise, the way he dressed, his coarse manners. He tried to fix his faults by wearing a suit. Even a vest. I had to laugh when he began holding his coffee cup with his pinky finger pointed in the air."

A sports writer who came into the Alamo regularly gave Jimmy two free tickets to a baseball game. "Although Jeannie wasn't the fan I was, she came along," Jimmy said. "Usually, when I have to do the buyin', I sit in the bleachers. This time, I have box seats right behind first base. In about the third inning, a pop fly is hit right in my direction. I'm about to catch it when Jeannie falls on my arm an' I drop the ball. So another guy sittin' behind us reaches out an' grabs it. I wanted to bawl Jeannie out but I suddenly realize that she pushes me because she's afraid the ball might hurt me. It was her way of showin' me that a good wife worries all the time. Maybe all she wanted was for me to answer back. But I just kept quiet. An' maybe that made her madder still about a lot of things."

Mildred Plowden lived in the same boarding house. She occupied a room with her mother, a former chorus girl who was now a floorwalker in Batterman's, a local department store. "I was only ten years old at the time we lived there," she said. "I suppose some of what I think I saw was actually told to me by my mother. Anyway, when I tossed a ball against the stoop or jumped rope, Mrs. Durante would tell me that she had a sick headache and that I must stop making so much noise. When I listened to the radio in the parlor, she'd always turn the dial to something she wanted to hear.

"On the other hand, Jimmy was just the opposite. He'd always pat me on the head and act as if he was pleased to see me. Not only would he watch me play ball or jump rope, but he'd join in. Sometimes he'd bring pie home from the place he worked. The next morning I'd find it in the icebox with my name written on the bag. I can't say this for sure, but I strongly suspect that Jimmy wanted to have children. I think it was Mrs. Durante who nixed the idea. Their being childless was an unexplained sorrow."

Jeanne resented sharing a kitchen and bathroom with strangers. She went apartment hunting and found a six-room flat on West Fifty-second Street. Jimmy felt that ninety-five dollars a month rent was much too expensive, and that the apartment was too large for only two people. He suggested that they rent out rooms. Their first boarder was Jack Roth, Durante's new drummer.

"Jimmy was an ideal landlord," Roth said. "Not only did he never dun me for the rent, but always made sure that my wallet had something in it besides my identification. Jimmy was like that with all the boys in the band. That's why we played our hearts out for him. At the start we called ourselves 'Jimmy Durante's New Orleans Jazz Five.' A few months later we changed the name to the 'Memphis Five.' The reason for the switch was due to Jimmy's modesty—he frowned on any kind of personal publicity. That was one of the big things Jeanne argued about. I can still hear her shouting, 'You always hide your head in the vermicelli!' She kept urging him to quit. Finally, he told Sam Sakerton that he was leaving. To make sure, Jeanne came along with him. Sam offered Jimmy a ten dollar raise if he'd stay. I think Schnozz was about to accept. But before he could reply, Jeanne took his arm and steered him outside. His face was full of surprise and anger. Another man would have walked out of that marriage. Not him. He was much too loyal!"

Most of Jimmy's friends felt that Jeanne Durante was

oblivious to Schnozzola's warmth. Writer Damon Runyon believed that the reason for continuing the marriage may have been due to Jimmy's unwarranted logic: "No women could possibly love me because of my ugly nose." As a result he was everlastingly touched and grateful that she had consented to marry him.

8

Still on the Cabaret Circuit

"**I** worked at the Alamo for six years," Jimmy told me.

"No," said Jackson. "It was longer than that. You've always been foggy about dates. I'll bet you don't even know when Columbus discovered America?"

"There you go with that extra year of schoolin' you had!" Jimmy said as he rolled out each word with mock intensity. "What difference does a couple of years make among friends. An' that's what we are—at least for right now!"

I was interviewing both of them at Durante's home which had numerous momentoes stacked up on a living room table. I fingered a chipped ash tray. "What's this?" I asked as I attempted to stop the argument.

"Funny you picked up that particular piece," Jimmy said. "It's from the Alamo. It got broken when a customer tosses it at a waiter for not bringin' his drink fast enough. Whenever I think about that place, I become neurologic because it taught me a lot about show business. I hadn't yet started talkin' full-time, but it was at the Alamo I begin jokin' around with the customers, an' start writin' songs."

His first one, "Remember the Alamo," was never published. It contained such immortal lines as:

I was never born in Texas,
But still I remember the Alamo.
It always gives me lots of memories,
But never do-re-me-dough.

Jimmy had better luck with one he wrote with Chris Smith, a popular songwriter, who was responsible for the hit, "You're In the Right Church But In the Wrong Pew." They collaborated on "Daddy, Your Mama Is Lonesome for You." The Triangle Music Company bought all rights for a hundred dollars.

In the weeks following his departure from the Alamo, Durante continued to compose songs. However, he felt the need of a steady paycheck now that he had a wife to support. He landed a piano playing spot at the Club Pizzazz, a darkly lit cabaret that had once been a stable. Very little cleaning had been done since the conversion, and the smell of horse manure was still evident. Club Pizzazz was on Eleventh Avenue and Thirty-first Street, close to Manhattan's West Side piers. The area, known as Hell's Kitchen, was regarded as one of the roughest sections in New York City. Most of the customers earned their living by working on the docks.

"They all looked as if they were ready to break you up in small pieces," said Jimmy. "And enjoy doing it. I don't say that because they was dock-wallopers. My cousin Frankie is one, but those who came to the Club Pizzazz were a pretty wild lookin' bunch. The only one that was different was a guy we used to call Lord Piccadilly."

The "Lord" possessed a highly starched Victorian accent, a carefully trimmed red goatee and a full-length black satin cape. There was a great deal of speculation as to why he had left his native land. The most prominent story was that he was the ne'er-do-well son of a titled father who had exiled him to the United States when he was caught hocking the family jewels. He was displaying his allegiance to England by attempting to live in the nineteenth century when it still ruled the waves.

Lord Piccadilly would smile benignly whenever Jimmy queried him about his heritage or mentioned the pawn shop theory. "That's quite a stimulating tale you profound chaps describe," the Lord would reply without agreeing or disagreeing. Each night, a little after midnight, he'd saunter into the Pizzazz and take a seat next to the piano. Regally, he'd order a "lager." Between the musical numbers, he'd engage Jimmy in involved conversations. It is questionable if either man understood the other. Nevertheless, they would talk on and on.

While Jimmy was performing at the Pizzazz, the club's porter, Stiff Barrows, was rushed to the hospital. Barrows, who was black, had suffered severe burns while tending the furnace. Several days later, Durante visited him. He found the porter sharing a small basement ward with about a dozen other black patients.*

Barrows, whose right hand had just been amputated, was lying in bed shivering from both pain and intense cold. Although it was in the middle of February, his sole cover was a dirty sheet. Jimmy summoned the nurse who told him to take his complaint to the front office. He did. The response was: "What are you, some kind of nigger lover?"

"Maybe that's what I am," Jimmy said. "In show business you learn pretty quick that people no matter what color or religion they are should be treated the exact same way.

"That night it was hard for me to be funny. But I didn't have too much time to think about it. The next day was Saturday and the boss of the Pizzazz fails to show up. Saturday is the busiest night for us, so I'm surprised. Me an' a few of the waiters an' some others wait, but no one comes to open up the place. I go around the next day, but it's the same thing—the boss had plain skipped. He still owes me for two weeks. I learn that everyone is in the same boat. It turns out that he's in debt to even his own mother!"

Jimmy's next job was at the Club Paradiso in East Harlem where he was a fill-in for the regular pianist who was serving a sixty-day prison sentence for beating up a customer. When the ex-convict returned, once again Durante was unem-

*At the time proper medical care for blacks was not only inferior, but scarce.

47

ployed. Jeanne suggested that he look for an acting part on Broadway. He tried. However, he always received the customary, "Don't call us, we'll call you."

In February of 1922, Durante landed a permanent job as the leader of a six-piece band at the Nightingale, a cabaret on Forty-eighth Street. "I was pretty happy." Jimmy said, "but they made me wear a soup-an'-fish suit, an' a fancy bow tie. As if that wasn't bad enough, Jeannie was in a tizzy because of a little gal down in the Nightingale by the name of Rose. Most men ain't angels. Me included. You know, sometimes, whether you mean anythin' by it, it's just flirtation, nothin' serious in it. This little gal down there I'm foolin' around with a little bit an' Jeannie happens to find out about it. Brother!

"After work I'd be flirtin' with that little gal an' I'd come home late an' tell Jeannie I'm trying' to make some extra dough by workin' after hours at a place my pal, Jimmy Kelly, runs on Sullivan Street in Greenwich Village. The tips I used to make at the Nightingale, I'd say was the extra pay. I got this awful habit of instead of tellin' the truth so as not to hurt anybody, I tell them little lies. After a couple of weeks, Jeannie finds out. I can't blame her for bein' mad. I tell her, 'There's nothin to it. Believe me. Nothin'!' Anyway, I quit seein' Rose. To make sure, Jeannie makes me come right home the minute I finish work. She calls up to make sure."

Not only did Jeannie keep close watch on him but when the Nightingale shut for the summer months, she and Jimmy went to Clear Lake in Northern California where her mother and new stepfather had a cabin. "Our nearest neighbor was maybe a mile away," Jimmy said. "That lake was over thirty miles long. There was nothin' else to do but go fishin'. I must of caught more then a thousand bass an' catfish. I tossed the ones I thought were female back into the water. I wasn't taken' no chances with any kind of dame!"

The Durantes returned to New York several weeks before the Nightingale reopened. The vacation trip had cost more than they had anticipated. Hoping to pick up some extra money, Jimmy asked around if anyone knew of one-night stands.

"Yeah, I just got a call from Freeport, Long Island," said one booking agent. "They want a trio for four nights starting tonight."

"What does it pay?"

"Forty dollars a man. They want a piano, a drummer, and a violin."

"Okay, I'll take it."

Durante knew that he could count on Jack Roth, his drummer. But he lacked a violinist. He walked over to the Gaiety Building on Broadway, a hangout for unemployed musicians. In the lobby he stopped a young man carrying a violin case.

"You workin'?" he asked.

"No."

"Want to make forty dollars?"

For the next four nights Durante, Roth, and the violinist played to enthusiastic audiences. When it came time to collect the pay, Jimmy learned that it had already been given to the violinist, who had quickly vanished.

"But you know that I'm the leader!" Jimmy protested.

"Who ever heard of a piano-player leader!" the owner of the Freeport cabaret said contemptuously.

"It's things like that," Jimmy said, "makes a person never to trust a guy who plays the fiddle." Two weeks later, Durante reported to the Nightingale. Fortunately, they didn't harbor any prejudices against a pianist leading the band. "But to make sure," said Jimmy, "I start tellin' more jokes—I wasn't takin' no chances." A sure laugh-getter was when he would suddenly look startled. "Stop the music!" he'd yell. "There's an assassin in this band. An' I think I know who just blew the wrong notes on purpose. It's the guy who blows the sax. He better watch his step!"

Another comical outburst that always received bursts of applause was when he'd spot a favored customer. The response was so great that he later used a variation of it in the speakeasy he owned. He'd shout:

> Here comes a good friend of mine,
> Sit him down at table nine.

See that you treat him very fine,
Because he's a good friend of mine.
Skeet, skat, skat, skat, skoo.

He was now earning ninety-five dollars a week. Enough,
Jeanne thought, to purchase a small house in Queens. One of
Bartolomeo's customers had a son-in-law who was a "bargain" lawyer. Jimmy engaged him to draw up a contract and
borrowed down-payment money from his father. The Durantes became the owners of a house that cost $4,355 and was
on a 40-by-60 foot lot. The house needed painting. Again,
Bartolomeo was helpful. This time he suggested the son of the
man who sold him combs and brushes. "He give you a good
price," Bartolomeo said. Jimmy wanted yellow. Jeanne, grey.
They had to compromise on the bargain painter's choice—a
color he had left over from a previous job—black!

When the Nightingale shut for the summer, Jimmy took a
temporary job at Green Lake in the Catskill Mountains.
Jeanne's mother had sent her a round trip railroad ticket to
visit her in California. Several times a week Jimmy received a
letter from his wife. The last line was usually the same: "I'm
crying my eyes out thinking of you." Early in July, she called
him at the Green Lake hotel at 3:30 in the morning.

Jimmy told Eddie Jackson about the incident. "I'm sound
asleep," he said, "when I hear a knock on the door. It's the
porter who tells me I got a long distance call from California.
Since it's still in the middle of the night, I'm plenty worried.
Then I remember that in California it's lots earlier. But even
if it's earlier, I run to answer the phone. I hear Jeannie's voice.

" 'Toots, toots,' I say. 'What's the matter?' She answers,
'Jimmy, you're not foolin' around with some other woman? I
get so lonely for you.' We talk for almost an hour. How that
gal Jeannie must love me—when she hears my voice it makes
her so happy she won't hang up."

In September, the Durantes were reunited. "We were now
livin' in our new house," Jimmy said. "It has everythin'. A
garden, back an' front doors, an' even a electric washin' machine that the other owner left for us. But I could tell Jeannie

wasn't feelin' too happy about it. Somethin' was troublin' her."

Eddie Jackson was now also employed at the Nightingale. The two friends frequently had dinner together. "I could feel that he was very worried about his wife." Jackson said. "He asked me for advice, but I didn't dare to tell him what I really suspected. Jeanne Durante acted that way because she realized that very soon, her husband would become famous and that she'd remain a nobody. Instead, I told him that it was probably connected to some women's problem like change of life coming early. I think he believed me, or at least wanted to."

Jimmy didn't have too much time for speculation. The Eighteenth Amendment to the U.S. Constitution had recently gone into effect. It prohibited making, selling, or transporting beer, wine, or liquor. It was rumored that the Nightingale was closing permanently. Many of the so-called "legitimate" cabarets were being replaced by the speakeasy.

9

Anatomy of a Speakeasy

Suddenly bootleggers, hijackers, high-powered motor cars, bulletproof vests, and machine guns were part of American nightlife. The illicit manufacture and distribution of liquor spread so quickly that law enforcement officers were powerless to suppress it. Instead, they overlooked what was happening or joined in to help. Gang wars and killings became so commonplace that only the more sensational ones made headlines.

They occurred with such rapidity that when the bodies of unimportant hoodlums were discovered, their deaths were relegated to back pages of most newspapers. Typical coverage was a very brief item that appeared in the New York *Telegram* when the body of a small-time bootlegger was found in an alley outside a Harlem speakeasy. Two lines were devoted to the incident: "Last Wednesday night Bruno Ross was shot to death outside of Harold's, an all night hotspot. Another statistic in the ongoing bootleg war." Most newspaper readers of the day could tell you instantly that the following bigwig names were connected to bootlegging: Murray the Camel Humphries, Ozario Scrooge Tropea*, Billy Spike O'Donnel, Sam Golf Bag Hunt, Jake Hymie Loud Mouth Levine, Jack Machine Gun McGurn.

Humorist Robert Benchley told his readers that it had become very necessary to have a descriptive nom de plume if you want to succeed in the liquor industry. "If you have three or more nicknames," he said, "you're certain to be elected to the board of directors. Look at Johnny Win, Place and Show Plunkett—he's vice president of one of the syndicates." Benchley once counted thirty-eight speakeasies on West Fifty-second Street between Fifth and Sixth Avenues.

New York City Police Commissioner Grover Whalen estimated that there were 25,000 in Manhattan alone. "They mushroom so fast," he said, "that it's difficult to keep track of them. All you need is a hundred dollars to start one up." Whalen was speaking of the "workingman's" speakeasy. This type was usually located in loft basements and remained open around the clock for the benefit of the man who felt the need of a shot before and after his ten hour shift. Packing cases served as the bar. Tables and chairs were relics that had been purchased at a rummage sale. Durante's cousin, Harry Ipolliti, owned several of this type. He offered to allow Jimmy to manage one. However, Ipolliti was deported when a printing press used to manufacture bogus ten dollar bills was discovered in his basement.

The second type was the "neighborhood" speakeasy where you could take your wife or girlfriend. It was a very friendly place—the bartender always knew your first name. However, unlike the corner saloon, there were no free lunches. To make up for it, drinks-on-the-house were issued several times a night. Wednesday was dish-giveaway and Saturday nights were devoted to group singing. A neighborhood speakeasy on the East Side was run by a pedicurist who administered free foot care at no additional cost.

The most profitable speak was called the "ritzy." It catered to corporation board members, Wall Street executives, and

*Ozario Tropea was one of the Alamo's steady customers. One Christmas Eve he mugged a Salvation Army Santa Claus. That's when Jimmy nicknamed him Scrooge. It stuck.

social register celebrities. It was also a haven for notorious gangsters. Responsible citizens found it thrilling to be seated next to mobsters and to join them in sneering at the law.

The ritzes were often located in Manhattan brownstones that formerly housed high society families. One wealthy grandam was so incensed by the constant ringing of her bell by revelers trying to locate a watering hole that she instructed her butler to post a sign on her front door, "No, this isn't! It's a private residence!" When she died, her heirs sold the house to a syndicate that planned to open a speakeasy. She might have been pleased to learn that the new owners gave their enterprise a dignified name: "The Pedagogical Night Club."

Many of the more successful speakeasies operated as private clubs: the Bombay Bicycle Club, Hinterland Hunting Club, Town and Country Club, Twenty-One Club.* The Montage and King Club was so exclusive that it had a club tie and its own song. Two of the lines were:

> You only pass this way but once,
> So drink, drink for the King.

These clubs claimed the liquor was imported stuff. It often was but the content was vigorously cut. Most owners doubled or tripled the brew with domestic liquor, water, and coloring. Texas Guinan, who was known as the queen of the illicit night clubs, boasted, "The suckers never can tell the difference!"

Purchase usually began in a nearby hotel room where buyer and seller arranged to meet. After dickering about price, cash would exchange hands. The seller would then take out a dollar bill from his wallet, tear it in half making sure it was done in zig-zag fashion. He'd keep one half for himself and give the other part to the buyer. A few days later a truck would deliver the bootleg liquor. The "bill-of-health" receipt was the torn dollar bill—if both halves matched perfectly, the drop was made.

---

*The Twenty-One Club still survives. Today it operates as a respectable, expensive restaurant.

Prohibition introduced a new vocabulary. A person who drank too much would become *blotto, soused, stewed, cock-eyed, pickled, zozzled, high, lit, ossified, polluted*. A federal liquor agent posing as a would-be speakeasy customer toured major cities. His mission was to learn how long it would take to purchase an illegal drink:

> New Orleans—35 seconds
> Detroit—3 minutes
> New York—3 minutes, 10 seconds
> Boston—11 minutes
> Atlanta—17 minutes
> Chicago—21 minutes
> St. Louis—21 minutes

Most speakeasies employed a spotter who was called "Mr. Eagle Eye." His job was to carefully scrutinize unknowns who approached the peephole. If he suspected you of being a government agent that he didn't think was on the payroll, he would summon the boss. However, the spotter would often be told not to worry because the stranger had been paid off.

Sunday sermons were regularly devoted to bootlegging. "In the Law's Pocket," was the title of one the Reverend Charles P. Levering of Brooklyn's St. Matthew's Baptist Church delivered to his congregation. Movingly, he said, "The law not only overlooks the bootlegger and the speakeasy owner, but is their faithful servant. The average policeman earns considerably more from these evil, sodden masters, than he does from the city. . . . He rests deeply in the devil's pocket. You and I must shred that pocket to pieces, so he can escape!"

Bishop Thomas Nicholson, President of the Anti-Saloon League, told his followers at the organization's biennial convention, "We are now in the greatest struggle since the Civil War for the effectuation of democracy." He then led them in a rousing song:

> Comrades, gird your swords tonight,
> For the battle is with dawn!

Oh, the clash of shields together,
With the triumph coming on!

Despite these vigorous opponents, it was not uncommon to find a prohibition agent sharing a bottle of Scotch with a bootlegger. Even the honest officer closed his eyes to violations. "What's the use?" said one of them who wore a sheet over his head when he testified before a Congressional committee. "I'll padlock some place. The owner complains to my chief who gives him permission to tear up the summons. A few days later the padlock is removed."

The most famous inspectors were Izzy Einstein and Moe Smith. Izzy was 5 feet 5 inches and weighed 230 pounds. His partner, Moe, was slightly shorter, but a few pounds heavier. The two were supposedly feared by speakeasy owners because of their strict interpretation of the law. Izzy, who had once appeared in amateur stage productions, felt he knew how to alter his appearance with makeup and an assortment of weird costumes. Posing as a professional baseball player, rabbi, jazz musician, garbage collector, he'd "manage" to get past the peephole.

Having gained entrance he'd order a drink. As soon as the waiter left the table, Izzy would pour it into a funnel that was concealed in the top pocket of his jacket which led into a rubber tube to a tiny bottle sewn into the lining. The evidence was then analyzed and subpoenas were issued. Few speakeasy owners were fooled by the disguises. They allowed Izzy his fun since they knew judicial authority was securely bought by their side. There were "bargain days" on which a large number of Prohibition Act cases were settled for very low fines. Izzy and Moe were finally discharged "for the good of the service."

It was difficult to properly supervise local prohibition agents when bootleggers operated freely in the nation's capital. During the Harding administration, 1625 K Street, which was known as the "President's Little Green House," was frequently used as a liquor distributing center. Cases of beer, wine, and whiskey were openly delivered by agents of the

Department of Justice. The availability of bootleg liquor was so widespread that even the very sober *Congressional Record* included a quote from one of Robert Benchley's columns: "Thank God for the bootlegger who made it possible for me to get out of these wet things and into a dry martini."

10

Club Durant

Jimmy was inadvertently plunged into this corrupt environment. "I keep tellin' Frank Nolan that I ain't got such a good head for business," he said. "He won't take no for an answer an' keeps right on buggin' me. So the next thing I know is I'm part owner of a booze joint."

Durante was replying to a question I had asked him about the Club Durant. For two years that speakeasy was one of the most popular "booze joints" in the Broadway area. Satisfied customers included gangster Legs Diamond, industrialist Alfred P. Sloan, producer Billy Rose, pugilist Jack Dempsey, philanthropist John Hay Whitney, writer Damon Runyon, department store owner Bernard F. Gimbel, movie star John Barrymore, and columnist Ed Sullivan.

Nolan, who had been head waiter at the Nightingale, recognized Jimmy's talents. "I knew right off he'd make a swell partner," he said. "I kept telling him that, but he wouldn't listen. I promised that we'd name the speak after him. Even that didn't make a dent."

"I'm unlucky in ownin'," Schnozzola protested. "The

58

house I got sprung a leak in the roof. My lawn mower busted a blade, an' our radio keeps groanin' like Lon Chaney."*

"This is different," Nolan said. "It's a sure thing!"

"Nothin' is for sure, not even death an' Texas."

"I tell you that we'll make a killing!"

"Then why don't you do it by yourself an' not have to share the profit?"

"Here I'm offering you a chance to become wealthy, and you keep on with silly questions!"

To get Nolan to cease pressuring him, Jimmy finally said, "Well, maybe it's not such a bad idea." The former head-waiter took that as an affirmative reply. Several weeks later, after a great deal of searching, he placed a deposit on a loft located above a used car salesroom at 232 West Fifty-eighth Street. To reach it, you had to climb a ladder and open a trap door.

"Only a mountain goat could come in that way," Jimmy said when he saw it.

"If we put in a partition for a hallway and build some stairs, we're in business," Nolan replied.

"That'll cost plenty. I'm not Rockinfellow!"

"We don't need much cash. Only a few hundred each—I'm sure that I can arrange an I.O.U. for the rest. We'll pay it off when we start raking the money in!"

"Okay! Okay! I know when I'm licked," Jimmy said. "But I want Eddie Jackson an' Harry Harris to each get a quarter share."

"Why do we need them?" Nolan asked.

"Jackson's been with me for years," Jimmy said. "An' he usually sings with Harris. That way we'll get free entertainment."

"Durante, you drive a hard bargain. Jackson and Harris are equal partners. Satisfied?"

* * *

---

*Actor Lon Chaney had just filmed *The Hunchback of Notre Dame*. As the badly deformed Quasimodo he was required to demonstrate his agony by constantly groaning.

Jeanne Durante tried to talk her husband out of it. "I don't want you messed up with bootleggers," she told him. "You'll only wind up in jail. Don't do it. I beg you!"

"The way she said those words got to me," he said. "I decided to tell Nolan the deal was off. But somethin' inside wouldn't let me back out. Where I come from, once you give your word, you never break it. But I didn't dare ask Jeannie for any of our savings."

Jimmy managed to borrow $700 from Frank Zaggarino, a Brooklyn nightclub owner. Nolan, Jackson, and Harris each scraped together similar amounts. The renovation was lots higher than Nolan thought. Fortunately, the contractor was willing to take a note; however, he wasn't in a hurry to finish the job, and alterations took a long time to be completed. While waiting, Durante performed nightly at the Club Royal, a speakeasy on East Fifty-second Street.

"Finally, Nolan tells me everythin' is ready," Jimmy said. "Zaggarino loaned us some booze an' food things for the kitchen. All we needed now was a big electric sign so we could open up. Nolan tried to talk me out of wantin' one. 'You shouldn't advertise a speak,' he says. But I want one. I don't want to be one of them owners who keep everythin' a secret. I don't want to have a sneakin' kind of a joint with no numbers on the door, an' where they gyp all the customers. When a guy comes back with a cop he can't prove what number he's been clipped at."

The sign maker agreed to take fifty dollars a week until the full sum of $350 was paid. He didn't know there was an "e" at the end of Jimmy's last name and wanted a hundred dollars more to add the extra letter. The four partners settled for "Club Durant."

A small kitchen had been built at the far end of the loft. There were twenty-five secondhand tables, seating 135 customers. The chairs didn't arrive until a few hours before the opening. The driver who delivered them had been given firm instructions to get ninety-five dollars in cash before he unloaded them.

"Ninety-five dollars!" said Jimmy. "I don't believe the four of us had a fin between us. What were we goin' to do, sit the customers on the floor? I was really frettin' when one of the waiters pipes up. He had a hundred dollars hidden under the carpet in his Harlem bedroom. Would that help us? My God, that man looked like the Chase National Bank in a bob-tailed coat an' apron. He rushes off to get the money an' the chairs move in."

A very tiny section of the loft was reserved for the band and floor show. "We had a four piece orchestra," said Jimmy. "Cornet, banjo, drums, an' piano. The dance floor was the size of a postage stamp. Things were so cramped that the waiters had to be on a diet so they could squeeze past. Nolan was to take care of the kitchen. Jackson, Harris, an' me, the entertainment."

"It was customary to lease out the checkroom and cigarette concessions," said Jackson. "They were valuable. Customers didn't seem to mind paying: a couple of dollars for a pack of cigarettes, ten dollars for a single rose, twenty-five dollars for a rag doll. Jimmy handed out both concessions gratis to a crippled girl named Edna. He told us, the poor kid is so crippled, she has to walk with two canes. How could I make her pay for the job? It would be worse then stealin' from the church poor box."

Durante's compassion was also evident in hiring other people. The man who opened taxi doors was usually in the employ of racketeers who would secure the rights from the speakeasy owner. They then would install a member of their gang to collect the tips which were quite sizeable. The Club Durant's doorman was a former waiter who had once worked at the Alamo. "He came down on hard times," Jimmy said. "Nobody would hire him when he got a bad case of the shakes."

Jimmy's sister, Lillian, composed a flyer inviting customers to the Club's grand opening on November 18, 1923:

You are cordially invited to the Club Durant
232 West 58th Street
(Three doors East of Broadway)
Entertainment Extraordinary Featuring
Jackson and Harris
The Two Hot Syncopators
and Broadway's Favorite
JIMMY DURANTE
and his Club Durant Orchestra
Mirth   Melody   Novelty

Despite the promise of mirth, melody, and novelty, few patrons climbed the stairs to Club Durant. "We was deader than
doornails," said Jimmy. "No one could charge us with sellin'
unlegal booze—we wasn't sellin' nothin'. It got so desperate
that Nolan announced he was goin' to fire the chef an' do all
the cookin' by himself. Harris just stared at the empty register
an' decides he doesn't want to be an owner any more. We all
felt the same way but were too mousy to say so. We was saved
by circumstances in the person of Lou Clayton."

Clayton had just lost $98,000 in a floating crap game. Start-
ing out with $300, he had run up his investment to a sensa-
tional high in forty-three hours of continuous play. Then his
luck changed. He called it quits when he was down to ten
dollars. Most people would have been devastated by that
gigantic loss. Not Lou Clayton. He had previously won and
lost astronomical pots.

Since the last gambling den was on West Fifty-eighth
Street, he wound up at the Club Durant, where he ordered a
double Scotch. While downing it, he complimented Jimmy
on his piano playing. Durante was flattered and offered to
play any song Lou wanted.

"Do you know 'Willie the Weeper?' Clayton asked.

"No, I never had the pleasure of meeting the gentleman,"
Jimmy responded.

Clayton was so amused with Durante's reply that he invited him to his table. It developed that he was a soft-shoe

dancer* and had once worked with Eddie Jackson. Jimmy called Eddie over. The three men sat in the virtually deserted nightclub until six the following morning. Jimmy told his new friend about the sad plight of Club Durant and that Harris wanted out. Three nights later the devil-may-care gambler returned with $1,000 to buy Harris's share.

*A type of tap dancing that didn't require metal taps on shoe soles. It was extremely popular in the early twenties.

11

Jimmy's Bestest Best Friend

"Eddie Jackson is my best friend," Durante said. "But Lou Clayton is my bestest best friend. For me, that guy would take the shirt off his back he's wearin' if I asked for it an' give it to me for nothin'."

"Jimmy's assumption may not be letter-perfect," said Clayton. "But it's authoritive." He loved to use multisyllable words. He was once enrolled in a mail-order school where one of the courses was: Application of Colorful Language for All Occasions. Upon receipt of a money order for twenty-five dollars he was awarded a degree. Proudly, he displayed the rumpled diploma he always carried.

"It's interesting that both Clayton and Jackson flaunt their academic background, and that Durante falls for it," said journalist Quentin Reynolds. "For my money, Schnozzola can more than hold his own. Nevertheless, he is in awe of their so-called scholastic accomplishments."

Clayton was born Louis Finkelstein. When he was thirteen years old, his father, who owned a small dry goods store in East Brooklyn, went bankrupt. The family was forced to

64

move to a cold water flat. Lou attempted to help out financially by working as an office boy in a Queens furniture factory. To avoid paying the three cent car fare, he'd hang on to the rear of the trolley. For several weeks his free transportation scheme worked but during a heavy ice storm he slipped. The accident resulted in a severe concussion, extensive internal bleeding, and badly crushed legs. An ambulance rushed him to St. Catherine's Hospital where doctors managed to save his life. They predicted, however, that he'd never walk normally again.

For five months he was kept under close observation. Card playing was his sole recreation; lumps of sugar stolen from the hospital kitchen were used in place of money. A fellow patient, Benevolent Charlie, who identified himself as a professional gambler, became the youngster's mentor. When Lou was discharged, Benevolent Charlie found him a sleep-in job cleaning horse stalls at the Sheepshead Bay race track. Sonny Swinton, another young employee, earned extra money by tap dancing for admiring bettors. They would toss coins at him while he pranced around. The faster he danced, the larger the haul.

Lou was envious and vowed he'd learn to become a hoofer. With Sonny as his teacher, he practiced regularly—often most of the night. Twenty months later he was able to shed his specially built-up shoes and began earning larger tips than Swinton. Once, both boys entered a dancing contest at a local theater. Sonny was awarded second prize—the first place winner was Lou Finkelstein. He changed his name to Clayton.

Eventually, he developed into a remarkable soft-shoe dancer. He had repeated engagements in most major cities—the Orpheum Circuit paid him $500 a week. Columnist Sidney Skolsky wrote, "This owner of smashed legs with a penchant for expensive, handmade suits, is truly a modern miracle. By firm resolution and discipline, Clayton has developed into one of vaudeville's finest soft shoe dancers."

Despite his success, Clayton's gambling fever remained strong and contributed to temporary setbacks. He teamed up with Ukulele Ike Edwards, a leading entertainer. Skolsky called the union, "An out-of-this world blending of two superb performers." The partnership was dissolved in a violent fist fight when Clayton insisted in participating in a major dice game instead of accepting a booking in Chicago. Fresh from that game he walked into the Club Durant.

"That Jimmy Durante had something special," Clayton once told Silverman. "Right off I knew that he was unique. Often an individual goes through life without experiencing loyal friendship—and I'm not referring to the carnal variety. From that very first time I met Jimmy, I was certain that my mission in life was to bring his distinctive talents to the attention of the world. Sure, we've had our ups and downs, but I remain convinced that he's an extraordinary human being."

Durante felt the same way, but phrased it differently: "When Lou came into my joint I knew at once we'd be like shoes an' socks. To me that man was dearer than gold. But I got to admit a few times the socks had small holes in it. Even so, Lou Clayton was one of the best things that ever happened to me."

Jackson and Nolan also recognized Clayton's talents. When he asked to be made president and treasurer of Club Durant, there weren't any objections. Like many gamblers, Clayton was an exaggeratedly honest man. At the end of the third week he handed each of his three partners $500. "That's just chicken feed profit," he said. "In the very near future there will be considerably more!"

The formerly empty speakeasy was now crowded with his cronies—Broadway performers, top executives, and mobsters. The latter liked his soft-shoe dancing so much, they obeyed his order to check their guns with Edna. When she complained about loaded guns being stored next to the hats and coats, the hiding place was switched to the long tin box the bartender kept his ice in. Jimmy used to refer to the guns as "frozen pistol puddin'."

The few who objected to handing over their weapons were treated to the Mickey Finn tablets Clayton always carried in his purple tuxedo jacket. Mumbles Trubino, who received his nickname long before the Dick Tracy comic strip became popular, was one of the protesters. He surrendered his piece reluctantly and spent the next hour griping about being forced to part with it. When he became obstreperous and started using foul language, Lou reached for one of his tablets. The moment Mumbles wasn't looking, he dropped it in his drink. The Mickey Finn took quick effect. As soon as Mumbles was snoring peacefully, Clayton dragged him to a waiting taxi and sent him home. A few days later the chastened gangster visited the club. This time, he politely relinquished his gun. He was so pleasant that Clayton treated him to a drink on the house. "Those punks have to know who is boss," Lou told Durante.

Even though Clayton weighed only 165 pounds, he had a well-deserved reputation of being very resourceful with his fists and equally handy with his ever present switchblade knife. "I think I'm strong," Jimmy said. "But compared to him, I'm a feather pillow. Why, I've seen that guy lick men three times his size an' weight. Every single day I thank God for sendin' him to the Club."

The customers seemed willing to pay the prices Clayton set: twenty-five dollars for a bottle of champagne, five dollars for a highball, a dollar fifty for a glass of beer. Chicken Soup á là Creole was ten dollars—the cost to prepare was thirty cents; Supreme Fried Smelts Versailles, fifteen dollars—the cost including tartar sauce was thirty cents. Lynnhaven oysters—wholesale cost eight cents apiece—a plate of six brought five dollars.

Sam Adler, alias Mr. Antoine the Chef, who had been hired by Clayton for $2,500 per year, was the club's most costly expenditure. He demanded a substantial raise when a newspaper story revealed that Mrs. Newton P. Astor's French chef received $25,000 for his cooking. Mr. Antoine ceased complaining when Clayton threatened to drop a Mickey Finn tablet into the Supreme Fried Smelts Versailles and make him eat it.

Richard Barthelmess, a leading Hollywood actor, was a frequent visitor. "It's a bargain," he said. "I'd gladly pay double the tariff just to see the show. Granted, the food is terrible, but the entertainment is superb."

Although Clayton was only five years older than Durante, the two men were more like father and son. "I know Lou's always lookin' out for me," said Jimmy. "So mostly I pay attention to what he tells me to do." Clayton's first change was to turn Durante into a comedian. Jimmy repeated what he had told Eddie Cantor when he was advised to leave the piano: "I couldn't do that. I'd be afraid they'd start laughing."

"That's exactly what I presume," Clayton replied. "Jimmy, you don't realize that you possess natural comic ability. Featuring your nose makes excellent sense. Let's take advantage of it!"

They did and it produced one of the few major quarrels the two men ever had. Clayton insisted on opening the Club Durant show with him reading a nose description he'd found in a Victorian book of etiquette: "The nose is the most prominent and noticeable feature of the face, as its functions are not all of the noblest kind, it especially behooves people who desire to be nice to avoid drawing attention to it. Consequently, all its requirements should be attended to in the quietest and most private manner as possible. It should never be fondled before company, or in fact, touched at any time, unless absolutely necessary. The nose like all other organs, augments in size by frequent handling. We recommend every person to keep his own fingers as well as those of his friends or enemies away from it."

Jimmy tried to talk Clayton out of using it. "Lou, please don't say those words," he pleaded. "People will think it has a dirty meaning. Particularly that part about the organ thing!" As usual Clayton's decision was final and Durante's nose became one of the greatest stage props to ever hit Broadway. Each night Clayton would carefully recite the Victorian nose definition, as a sheepish Jimmy cringed and continued to protest.

Durante: It's only my nose.

Clayton: Oh, then I've struck oil.

Durante: I already told you, it's only my nose!

Jackson: Maybe the man's right.

Clayton: Ladies and gentlemen, step right up to autograph the eighth wonder of the world.

Once, Jack Dempsey, the heavyweight boxing champion, attempted to do that. In the midst of signing his name, he quickly jumped back. "It's alive!" he shouted. "Run for your lives!" The jokes that followed were equally bewhiskered, but the audience roared as they listened to Jimmy's hoarse East Side voice.

Durante: Can you guess who I am?

Clayton: You're Jimmy Durante, the well-known man about town.

Jackson: Lou, you're right. It's the man with the magnificent nose, let's ask him a question.

Clayton: Mr. Durante, do you file your nails?

Durante: Naw! I just cut them off an' throw them away.

Clayton: Mr. Durante, do you speak French?

Durante: Si. Si.

Jackson: But that's Spanish.

Durante: How do you like that? I speak Spanish, too.

Clayton: Mr. Durante, where are you going tomorrow?

Durante: I'm goin' to an insane asylum.

Jackson: An insane asylum?

Durante: Yeah, I'm gonna get me a ravin' beauty.

"For some strange reason the joke about raving beauties always got the most laughs," Jackson said. "Especially from the ladies. They would become hysterical when Jimmy delivered that line. Old lady Webster actually cackled!"

Seldom did a woman visit the Club Durant unescorted. Evelyn Grayson Webster was one of the few exceptions. She was a rich elderly widow whose late husband had helped found the National Lumber Corporation of America. Several times a month Mrs. Webster's chauffeur would drive her to West Fifty-eighth Street. She was always given the same front table. One night the club was so crowded she had to share it with a young naval ensign and his wife who was very pregnant. Suddenly, the expectant mother started shrieking, "My baby is coming!" She moaned so loudly that Jimmy ran over. Mrs. Webster, who had done some volunteer work in a maternity clinic, told him labor looked so advanced that a doctor might not get there in time. She decided to do the delivering herself with Durante acting as her assistant.

They didn't have much opportunity to serve as doctor and nurse because the infant arrived a few moments later—a boy weighing 7 pounds 5 ounces. The grateful parents named him James Evelyn in honor of the two people who had been instrumental in bringing their new son into the world. Damon Runyon wrote a short story about the incident. Clayton sold a version of it to Hollywood.

As soon as third act curtains were lowered on Broadway shows, many of the actors appearing in them gathered at the Club Durant for a relaxing drink. Jimmy was awed by their presence and gave his bartender a standing command: "Give them only the good stuff—and don't be stingy!"

Among the late night callers were Alfred Lunt and his wife, Lynn Fontanne, who were appearing in *The Guardsmen*. Also Will Rogers and W. C. Fields, the stars of the Ziegfeld Follies. After downing his third drink, Fields would insist on becoming part of the entertainment. As the customers cheered him on, he'd perform a sketch from the play—a very tired drug store owner attempting to snooze on his back porch.

"One night he actually fell asleep," Jimmy said. "He looked so comfortable that I didn't want to wake him up. So to make sure he wouldn't be disturbed, I told the customers to stop making noise."

Fields was often accompanied by Babe Ruth. Baseball's celebrated home run hitter feared that newspaper photographers would show him guzzling an alcoholic beverage. To prevent it, Jimmy instructed Club Durant waiters to serve Ruth's drink in a soda bottle.

"I knew the Babe from my Coney Island days," Durante said. "One time when he was there I watched him eat two dozen hot dogs an' drink a whole gallon of lemonade. Like lots of people he used to rub my nose for luck. The last time he did, he rubbed it three times. An' what do you think happened—that the next day he hit three homers? No! He struck out three times in a row. It was humiliatin'."

After locking the club door—usually at 8:00 or 9:00 A.M., Clayton would invite Jimmy and two other players to join him in a round of golf. Durante tried it but lost interest in the game when he learned his score was routinely over a hundred despite some subterfuge. Each time he'd hit a ball into the rough, he'd sneak back to the fairway and drop another ball. Clayton, who shot in the low seventies, knew that his friend was cheating, but he let him get away with it—he was too busy betting on each hole with the other two players.

During the Club Durant period, Jimmy's income kept increasing. He bought Jeanne an automobile, added a fireplace to the house, and paid off the mortgage. However, Jeanne wasn't happy and took to solitary drinking. She became sullen and withdrawn. Her hostility to Jackson and Clayton was very evident. "I don't think she spoke to me more than a hundred words in the later years," Jackson said. "And none of them were complimentary. I finally asked her, 'Jeanne, why aren't you friends with me? Did I do something?' And she looked at me, hurt and bitter. 'You and Lou Clayton took my love away from me,' she said."

The Three Sawdust Bums
Are Back on Broadway

Sime Silverman, editor of *Variety*, was Club Durant's most ardent fan. "Clayton, Jackson and Durante are the best sizzling, stimulating and satisfying show on Broadway," he said. "I warmly recommend your going to the Club Durant to catch the Three Sawdust Bums."

A few weeks after this glowing praise the Club Durant was padlocked for dispensing liquor. There were several conflicting stories concerning the forced closing:

- A rival speakeasy owner who resented their competition insisted that the law step in.
- Club Durant didn't pay for protection and a mobster chieftain decided to teach other owners that bribes and muscle money were very necessary if you wanted to stay in business.
- A rash of recent newspaper editorials condemning the laxity in speakeasy law enforcement shamed authorities into singling out a popular illicit nightclub.

The truth may be that a jealous Jeanne Durante was the culprit. "I don't want to point a finger at Jimmy's wife," Jackson said. "But I strongly believe that she was the one who started the ball rolling by handing out a lot of private facts. Her motive might have been so she could get back at Clayton and me, or plain jealousy that Jimmy was becoming famous. Or that she was a very sick lady. Maybe all three? Whatever it was, it shut us down but good."

It happened when two strangers approached the Club Durant doorman. He didn't recognize them and refused entrance. They demanded to see Durante. "Jimmy, old pal, it's so good to lay eyes on you again," one of them said when he appeared. "How's your brother Al and your sister Lillian?"

"Those sure were good times we had in Public School 114," the other man said. "Remember when a baseball landed on your head? Or the Fourth of July when your father's barber pole was found on the roof of Mrs. Perina's house?"

"Yeah, it's good to see you fellows," Jimmy said as he shook hands with both men. He told them to follow him upstairs where they were seated at a choice table and immediately served Scotch highballs.

"There's something about those two that doesn't look kosher to me," Clayton whispered.

"Those guys know me from the time I was a little kid," Jimmy replied. "They are two of my best friends. They even know my whole family." The next day, padlock proceedings were started. Jimmy's "childhood friends" were liquor inspectors.

"I apologized all over the place for not taking Lou's advice about those guys," Jimmy said. "But you know what? He wasn't even sore. All he did was shake his head a little. 'Jimmy,' he tells me, 'you trust everybody. Me, I'm the opposite. I trust no one—except you. You're too good-natured and too sentimental to double-cross anyone.'"

That's when Durante gave him a photograph of himself which he inscribed: "To my dear pal and partner, Lou, death will never us part."

* * *

A remark Jimmy made at the termination of Club Durant furnished a Hollywood writer with one of the most memorable lines ever uttered in a movie. It was the reply Claude Rains made in *Casablanca* when a Nazi officer ordered him to find a reason to shut Rick's cabaret. "I'm shocked to find out that gambling is going on here," Rains said as he suavely pocketed his winnings. Years before a writer who worked on the film overheard Durante say innocently, "And all the time I thought they was drinkin' sasperilla."

Several days following the Club Durant's closing in October 1925, Clayton accepted a week's engagement for them at Minsky's burlesque, which occupied the sixth floor of the National Winter Garden on Second Avenue and Houston Street. After two shows, Jimmy complained that he had suddenly come down with a bad case of pleurisy and couldn't perform.

"We went on without him," said Jackson. "However, I don't think sickness was the real reason he bowed out. True, nightclubs can be pretty spicy, but watching a woman strip in public was just too much for him."

Durante's brief burlesque appearance wasn't a total waste—for years he entertained his friends with his version of the candy butcher's spiel. Jimmy required a cane and derby for his impersonation. He'd cock the hat over his left eye, point the cane, and begin reciting. I asked him to do it for me. He was very willing:

"Ladies an' gentlemen, this misfortune is your good fortune. Because of havin' fallen on hard times, a well-known person who prefers to remain not known has asked me to sacrifice his priceless French postcard collection. His catostroke is your gain. So for this performance only, I'm gonna sell a set of six of these stimulatin' cards for the insignificant sum of only one dollar. But that ain't all. I'm also throwin' in a box of absolutely free bonbons—that's French for delicious, chewy candy. An' that's still not all. Call me crazy, but I'm also givin' away absolutely free a sixteen ounce bottle of imported French perfume. An' hidden in many of these perfume bottles is a gift of twenty American dollars. You can be one of the lucky winners. So reach down in your wallet for one measly dollar bill. I've just got enough for the first lucky customers."

Irving Berlin once said after listening to it, "Schnozzola was so delightful that I tried setting it to music. I didn't, but it wasn't from the lack of trying."

Eventually Clayton found other work for the trio at the Dover Club, a speakeasy at Fifty-first Street and Sixth Avenue. He asked for $3,000 a week—was offered $1,750. "That's not nearly enough," he said.

"We only do $3,000 business here, tops," said the owner, who was known as the Quaker because he'd start vibrating the moment money was discussed.

"You've got to raise the ante if you want us to come here," Clayton told him.

"Tell you what I'll do. $1,750 plus fifty percent of anything over $10,000 business."

"You're a robber, but it's a deal." The Quaker was so pleased he allowed Durante to place an ad in several New York newspapers. Again, Jimmy's sister, Lillian, wrote it:

Back Home from Gay Paree—Lou Clayton
From Liberty, New York—Eddie Jackson
From the West—Jimmy Durante
From Corona, L.I.—the help
New piano keys   New Electric Bulbs   New Bus Boy
Come and get a load of us
The Three Sawdust Bums Are Back on Broadway
And the Dover's Got them.

The first week they appeared, the Dover took in $18,000. Quaker tried to settle for the $3,000. Clayton demanded getting what had been promised. After a lengthy discussion the Three Sawdust Bums were given sixty percent ownership of the club. They would provide the entertainment and the Quaker would handle the business side.

"Except the cash register," Clayton said. "That will be my job!"

Jimmy continued to be the mainstay of the act. Clayton and Jackson would feed him lines and he'd deliver surefire laughs. A very reliable routine was for one of them to say, "Schnozzola, why don't you make yourself comfortable and stay awhile?"

"I don't mind if I do." Durante would reply. Then he'd remove the raccoon coat he was wearing. Underneath was another fur coat. He'd peel that off, and then several suits, sweaters, shirts, and ties. When he was down to a single pair of longjohns, he'd carefully scrutinize his surroundings while whistling, 'A little Bit of Whiskey Will Make Me Warm, and a Lot Will Make Me Hot.'*

"Every performance was different," said Silverman. "Jimmy would become bored doing exactly the same thing twice. One night he held a compass as he paraded around in his underwear. 'Please pull the window shades down,' he whispered. 'I don't want to give no free looks at this magnificent body.'

"Yes, they are silly gags. If someone else offered them I'd probably walk out with disgust. But it's different when Jimmy does it—the touching and abashed grins and looks when he delivers those lines is outstanding theater. In my days I've been privileged to see most of the great comedians—he's tops!"

John Barrymore was another Durante admirer. The legendary actor was reported to have said, "Jimmy, some day you should play *Hamlet*."

"None of them small towns for me," Durante replied. "It's New York or nothin'!"

One night Clarence Darrow and John T. Scopes came to the Dover to celebrate their victory in the famous "Monkey Case." They were visiting New York to attend a reception that had been given in their honor. Scopes, a biology instructor in a Tennessee public school, had been charged with defying a new state law which forbid teaching any theory

---

*A song that was popular at the time.

that denied the creation of man as told in the Bible. The case received tremendous attention because the former Democratic Presidential Candidate, William Jennings Bryan, represented Tennessee against the distinguished liberal attorney Clarence Darrow. The law was reflection of the revival of religious fundamentalism following World War I.

"A customer who was more then a little drunk creeps over to the table those two gents are sittin' in," said Jimmy. "He pretends he's a monkey. Keeps scratchin' himself an' gruntin'. Soon the whole place is doin' the same thing. That's when I start playin' on the piano the 'Star-Strangled Banner.' Like I figured, everybody stands up an' the gruntin' is all over."

Jimmy always observed his father's birthday by taking him out to a fancy restaurant and giving him expensive presents. During the Dover run it once was a gold wristwatch. A few days later Jimmy learned that Bartolomeo had returned the gift for a refund. He rushed over to his father's house to learn the reason.

"Pop, when I gave it to you, you sounded as if you liked it."

"*Giacoma*, it very nice. But I don't want to sit in church with a umbrella."

"What's an umbrella got to do with the wristwatch?"

"The church roof got holes in it."

Jimmy realized it was difficult to argue with such logic. He was used to it. Every month he gave his father a sizeable check—it was usually endorsed by the parish priest.

Clayton, Jackson, and Durante stayed at the Dover for two and a half years. During that period Quaker and the Three Sawdust Bums divided a profit of more than a half of a million dollars. This amounted to about $150,000 apiece—on which, of course, no tax was paid.

"That was a whole lot of money in those days," Jimmy said. "But Jeannie didn't want me to be a speakeasy owner no more. The poor kid was afraid I'd get arrested or even somethin' worse."

At the time a frequent gangland practice was to threaten nightclub owners. Unless they paid a sizeable sum—

protection money—they would be kidnapped, or their club wrecked—or both. Jimmy received a menacing letter: "If you don't come across with $25,000, you will be snatched and made very uncomfortable."

Clayton was furious when he was shown the note. Immediately, he sought out the identify of the sender from his underworld contacts. They told him that Mad Dog Coll, a member of the Dutch Schultz bootlegging mob, was behind the intended snatch. Unarmed, except for his switchblade, he located Coll in a Bronx hideout. "If anybody dares lay a hand on Jimmy Durante, I swear that I'll kill him!" Clayton said.

Coll knew that he wasn't kidding. Mad Dog had learned that the soft shoe dancer was a man of his word and a personal friend of Schultz. He backed off. When word of the backdown reached Broadway, Benevolent Charlie remarked, "Don't ever go up against Lou Clayton. He'd fight to a draw with the devil!"

Soon after the threatened kidnapping, the Durantes went to Clear Lake, California, for a holiday. Jeanne appeared to be in a happy mood and seemed to enjoy preparing the fish Jimmy caught. She went out on a shopping spree and bought him a new pole, a wicker fishing basket, and a Izaak Walton jacket that Schnozzola said was guaranteed to make the fish act more respectful.

The woman who cleaned their cabin was known as "Mrs. Calamity Howler." She read tea leaves and each morning she'd insist on telling Jimmy's fortune. He learned that he'd shortly inherit a large fortune but promptly lose it to gangsters; he'd buy four tires which would all go flat at the same time; he'd have to wear a red woolen scarf to protect his health which could deteriorate from too much piano playing.

"I received a picture postcard from Jimmy," Jackson said. "It had a gorgeous beach scene. On the other side he wrote, 'Me and Jeannie are resting and feeling great and eating lots of fish. Just got the greatest idea for a fortune telling skit. Can't wait to tell you and Lou about it.'"

In March of 1927, the Three Sawdust Bums started working at the Parody Club on East Forty-eighth Street for $3,000 a week. A fortune-telling skit was added to their routine. It was well received. Jimmy assumed the role of the eccentric sooth-sayer whose predictions were even wackier than those he had heard in Clear Lake. With frenetic head bobbing he'd walk out to the audience and read palms.

"We never knew what to expect," said Dr. Benjamin Gilbert, a Parody Club trumpet player who later became a physician. "He told one very slender man that he would be given solid gold bars for every pound he weighed. Jimmy advised the man to start taking Sawyer's Extract—a patent medicine based on lard—to build up his heft. To one high society investment banker he said that his palm revealed he was rapidly slipping from the social register because it had been discovered that his grandmother had taken in washing."

During the daytime, Gilbert was a student at the New York Medical College attached to Flower Hospital. Promptly at 7:30 P.M. he'd shed his white uniform for a tuxedo and start tootling a trumpet. When Johnny Hodge, one of the Parody Club owners, discovered the young man had inserted his anatomy lecture notes between sheets of music, he was enraged.

"You're fired!" he shouted.

"If he goes," said Jimmy. "I go, too!"

"And if Jimmy is out," said Jackson. "So am I!"

"That goes double for me," said Clayton. "I depart the moment Jimmy starts to exit!"

Gilbert stayed. A few days later, however, the dean of the New York Medical College happened to visit the club. He gave the would-be doctor the option of choosing medicine or continuing to blow the horn. Once again, Durante intervened. In his own quaint vernacular he pointed out that the spiritual release of music would surely contribute to Gilbert's becoming an excellent physician. Gilbert was allowed to continue his studies as well as working at the Parody. The following June, Schnozzola and Lou Clayton attended his graduation. The young man was named class valedictorian. In his commencement address, the brand new M.D. said, "Without Jimmy Durante's constant help I certainly wouldn't have finished school. He's the one that deserves this honor."

Clayton told the Parody club audience about Gilbert's medical success and how it had been made possible by Durante. Everyone applauded. In typical fashion, Jimmy hung his head and began singing his latest composition, "Again You Turnsa." The Republican National Committee, meeting in Kansas City, Missouri, had adopted the song. A spokesman said it reflected the turnabouts of the Democratic Party and that Herbert Hoover, their nominee, was above such things.

Jimmy, who supported Al Smith, Hoover's opponent, protested. "Everybody knows my songs don't knock nobody for real," he said. "They only lift up people like the one I just wrote about Lindbergh the flyer."

Joe Frisco, a comedian whose unique stuttering was a Broadway legend, was appearing at the Club Eighteen on West Fifty-second Street. In between numbers he'd come to see Schnozzola perform. He urged him to sing it. Jimmy didn't need too much encouragement.

> Lindy flew across the ocean blue,
> Makin' proud both me an' you.
> Hail to Lindy the number one,
> A goal for every mother's son.

When Durante returned to the dressing room, Frisco followed. "J-J-Jimmy," he whispered. "If L-L-Lindy hears th-th-that song, m-m-maybe he'll fly r-r-right back to P-P-Paris. It st-st-st—it's n-n-not so g-g-good." Schnozzola took Frisco's advice and never publicly sang it again.

13

King of the Palace

Most comedians felt they hadn't arrived until they played two-a-day at New York's Palace Theater. The Palace was regarded as the cathedral of vaudeville. Durante was no exception. He kept begging Clayton to get them a booking. "We'd have had a shot earlier," Jackson said. "But Lou always demanded more dough than they were willing to shell out. So we waited. It got so tense that Jimmy would have settled for the opening act. That was usually kept for trained animals—the worst spot on the billing."

Their opportunity finally came in late winter of 1927 when comedienne Fanny Brice took ill. The Palace needed a replacement and grudgingly agreed to Clayton's terms: $5,500 a week. The Three Sawdust Bums were scheduled to be on the stage for thirty minutes but the enthusiastic patrons refused to let them leave—the trio performed for an hour and a half. That first week they broke the Palace's attendance record that had been established by Beatrice Lillie, the British comedy star. They were held over for three additional weeks.

The audience response was so overwhelming that they soon became frequent Palace headliners. On one of their subsequent appearances they introduced the wood routine that was considered their greatest number. Jimmy had read an advertisement of the National Lumber Manufacturer Association which said that wood had been responsible for our country's glorious past. This inspired him to write a skit about the virtues of lumber. He recited it to the tempo of Rudyard Kipling's poem, "Boots":

> Without wood there'd be no America.
> No ships to bring the Pilgrims across the ocean,
> No log cabins,
> No school houses,
> No churches,
> No covered wagons,
> No railroad ties,
> No cigar store Indians,
> No nothin'.

When he finished his soliloquy, Clayton and Jackson helped him carry in some wood products: a cedar chest, parts of a rosewood harpsichord, a birchbark canoe, a broken mahogany grandfather clock, bowling pins, a rolltop desk, and an outhouse. The act reached a climax when Jimmy held up a set of false wooden teeth. "These choppers," he said, "once belonged to George Washington, the uncle of our country."

The theater critic for the New York *Telegram* called the wood act, "Sheer pandemonium genius that kept the audience shouting for more. . . . It's difficult to ignore Jimmy Durante who has suddenly become King of the Palace."

At one matinee, however, a man sitting in the front row shouted, "Hey Big Nose, why don't you use your schnozzle for a prop? It's made of wood!" He began pelting Jimmy with spitballs and peanut shells. Clayton jumped off the stage, climbed over some orchestra members, and was on the verge of belting the kibitzer. He was stopped by Durante and Jackson who had followed him. Ushers tried to restore order, but before they could the police arrived.

"Can you imagine that guy?" Jackson said. "He was the one who wanted to prefer charges. But Jimmy calmed him down with some sweet talking. He told the man that he looked like a pretty smart person. He kept buttering him up. 'You sure know a thing or two,' Jimmy said. 'But my nose is real flesh and blood. Sometimes it even bleeds when someone picks it. Just feel for yourself but don't do no pickin.' That did it and a few seconds later the troublemaker began laughing and even shook Lou's hand."

While playing the Palace, the trio continued to perform at the Parody Club. "Not to be too exhausted we decided to stay at a hotel in Times Square," said Jackson. "Me and Jimmy shared a bedroom. Clayton insisted on a separate one. As soon as we checked in, Jimmy would telephone his wife. One time it was well past midnight when he was able to make the call. There wasn't any answer. Fifteen minutes later he tried again, but still no Jeanne. Three more calls were unanswered. 'I'm goin' home!' Jimmy said. 'Something's wrong!' I went along."

They managed to find a taxi that would take them to Queens. When they arrived, Jeanne's car was in the driveway and all the house lights were on. Jimmy was so unnerved that he kept dropping the key. Jackson had to open the door. Jeanne was sprawled out on the living room floor. She was unconscious. An ambulance was immediately sent for. The examining doctor said that she had passed out from excessive drinking, but would sleep it off.

"The next morning she acted as if nothing had happened," Jackson said. "Jimmy told me that neither he nor Jeanne ever mentioned it again, but you could tell he was plenty upset. Oh, he continued to be a sensational performer. However, the minute he left the stage he'd head for a telephone."

Several weeks later the trio was offered a lucrative out-of-town vaudeville assignment. The Sawdust Bums would receive $5,500 a week to perform in the midwest. Clayton and Jackson were delighted. Not Jimmy. "I can't leave Jeannie alone," he protested. "So the deal has to be off!"

"It came back on," said Jackson. "And all because of her. I think she acted that way due to the blackout—it must have scared her. Ordinarily, she would object whenever Jimmy had to spend a night away from her. This time she actually forced him to go. He didn't want to. Finally, he agreed. Only after he arranged for Jeanne's mother to visit while he was gone. Even then, he called home every single day—sometimes twice a day."

The tour was very successful. At each theater, Standing Room Only signs were posted. The jokes they used had been recycled again and again but it didn't seem to matter. It was Jimmy's combined qualities of naivety and impudence that drew the frenzied applause. Columnist Walter Winchell who saw them perform in Cincinnati said that he possessed the "contagious excitement of a naughty boy . . . without Schnozzola's bang-up style most of the gags would receive the Bronx cheer."

Clayton: Jimmy, what's a fiance?
Durante: A lady that's engaged to be married.
Jackson: That's exactly right. Now tell us what a fiasco is?
Durante: That's easy. It's the guy who is goin' to marry her.

Durante: I put a frame on the first dollar I ever earned.
Clayton: Jimmy, that shows fortitude. How much money do you have now?
Durante: Fifty cents. I had to pay fifty cents for the frame.

Durante: See the watch I'm wearin'? I paid plenty for it. It's imported.
Clayton: Swiss, I presume. What's its movement?
Durante: Back an' forth from the pawnshop.

In Chicago, Al Capone came to see the show. He liked it so well that he placed a specially built car at their disposal. When Schnozzola mentioned how much he admired the automobile, the gang lord offered to make him a present of it. Jimmy turned the offer down, saying his garage back home couldn't accommodate such a large car.

"Jimmy's singing voice was ideal for vaudeville," said *Variety's* Sime Silverman. "Volume counted for much more than sheer melodic ability and he was wise enough to spot it. He loved the cheap, wholesome entertainment this medium provided for people who didn't have much money."

During the vaudeville engagements Durante loved to listen

to his fellow performers discuss past accomplishments. "Believe me kid," said one old acrobat. "I always knocked them dead. Every night the cash customers made me do an Eddie Leonard. It got so that even our Gunga Din refused to go out for coffee so he could watch me."

Jimmy discovered that vaudevillians had a language of their own. Some of the more popular expressions were:

Eddie Leonard—Doing an encore.

Gunga Din—A person who ran errands.

Fish—An act that laid an egg.

Brodie—An act that laid two eggs.

Little Boy Blue—Being given notice.

Chooser—Performer who steals material.

Big Battle Axe—Manager or owner of the theater.

Little Battle Axe—The owner's wife.

Excess baggage—A nonprofessional wife traveling with her husband.

Chestnut—An audience that refuses to applaud.

Morgue—An empty house.

Mary's Lamb—A kid act.

Guttenburg—Clothes an actor carries in his trunk.

Houdini—Ad-libbing or getting out of tight spots.

Lillian Russell—A class act that elicits critics's praise.

Tony Pastor—Thoroughly clean act.

Alice In Wonderland—Dreaming about the big time.

Mary Malted—Birthday party.

The night of the final performance in Milwaukee a telegram arrived requesting them to play a week in Minneapolis. They accepted, but Jimmy never forgot the experience. "Who booked us into Minneanopolisa?" he asked his partners. "It musta been an enemy!"

14

"We Bombed in Minneanopolisa"

"That stand in Minneapolis really upset him no end," Jackson said. "For the life of him he couldn't figure out why all those people didn't like him. Thank God, Gracie Allen and George Burns, who had headlined the bill the previous week, stayed on to catch our act. They were the only ones in the audience that laughed in the right places."

Usually, there would be thunderous applause when Jimmy finished singing "I Can Do Without Broadway, but Can Broadway Do Without Me?" This time the reception was quite different. "Minneapolis can do without Clayton, Jackson and Durante," wrote a local theater critic. "If last night indicated what they can do, Broadway is more than welcome to them."

Eddie Foy, who appeared regularly in vaudeville with his wife and seven young children, had a similar experience in Minneapolis. "As soon as the curtain went up," he said, "I stared shrewdly at my wife and all those kids. Then I winked as I repeated the line that always drew big howls in the other cities: 'If I ever decide to move out here, this place will instantly become a huge metropolis!' Nobody in the entire house laughed. My joke had laid a gigantic goose egg!''

Phil Silvers, who went on to fame as the noncom con artist in television's "Sergeant Bilko," was another Minneapolis detractor. The wily comedian whose signature was rolling his eyes through black, lenseless horn-rimmed glasses said, "Everytime I played there I felt they just didn't want to sit on their hands, but sit on me!" Durante and Silvers once started a "Don't play Minneapolis club."

Years later Jimmy was still concerned about the adverse reception he had received there. After being introduced to Senator Hubert H. Humphrey, who had formerly been mayor of Minneapolis, he told him the sad story. The following week Humphrey sent Durante a written apology on official U.S. Senate stationery: "The good people of Minneapolis made one bad mistake in an otherwise glorious past when they failed to recognize your genius. Schnozzola, please give us another chance. Do come back to entertain us. I personally guarantee that this time things will be very different."

When The Three Sawdust Bums returned to New York in the fall of 1928, they began working at the Silver Slipper, a brand new speakeasy on Forty-eighth Street. Ten days later it was padlocked for selling liquor. A rumor heard on Broadway said that the real reason for the closing was that Big Bill Duffy, the Silver Slipper's frontman, had angered local bootleggers by buying his supply of contraband hootch from out-of-towners.

The trio moved to Les Ambassadeurs, several blocks to the north. Larry Fay, one of the owners, also operated a bookie parlor and a rum-running trucking business whose speciality was outwitting the Canadian Border Patrol. Although his illegal activities had earned him a small fortune, he was well known for his skinflint tactics. When Jimmy had to have a rectal operation at New York's Midtown Hospital, Fay insisted that each evening an ambulance bring him back to the club so that he could continue with the act. Schnozzola was willing, but an irate Clayton yelled, "Jimmy don't move out of that hospital until he's good and well!"

Durante stayed in the hospital for five days and rested at home for two more weeks. "Nobody dared bother him," said Jackson. "Lou saw to that. But Fay remained angry until Jimmy was well enough to go back to work. When he did, he found exactly the same place, but the club had a new name. It was now called the Rendezvous. The reason for the change was due to the son of a high-up government official being robbed in front of Les Ambassadeurs. Fay wanted to avoid bad publicity."

Durante complained about the conversion to his audience. "Just when I learn how to pronounce Les Ambassadeurs," he said, "they go an' change it to another hard word. I'm mortified!"

In spring of 1929, The Three Sawdust Bums were hired by Florenz Ziegfeld for his new musical comedy, *Show Girl.* It was about a theatrical romance that takes place backstage. Ruby Keeler had the starring role, and Schnozzola played a harassed property man with Clayton and Jackson as his assistants. On opening night, Ruby's new husband, Al Jolson, who was then considered the country's leading male pop vocalist, rose out of his seat and serenaded his bride with a song that had been intended for Durante. George Gershwin had written the song, "Liza," for Keeler's tap dancing. Monty Wooley was the director. He thought it would be amusing to have Jimmy sing it.

For a moment Jimmy was speechless when he heard Jolson croon his number. Then he lay down on the stage and said, "Everybody wants to get into the act, so I might as well take a rest in the meantime."

Walter Winchell, writing in the New York *Daily Mirror,* told his readers about it. "Lou Clayton and Eddie Jackson are super in *Show Girl.* But the superest of them all is Schnozzla Durante who is an inspired, gilt-edged madman. Last night Jolson found it out."

Jimmy received the show's loudest applause when he recited a poem he had just composed. At each performance the lines varied. "I got a memory that forgets in a hurry," he explained. Here's one of his versions:

I like a one-room house, you like a two-room, three-room, four-room, or more house.

I only got a one-room house.

An' if you ask me the reason, it's because I don't want a two-room, three-room, four-room, or more. So keep your two-room, three-room, four-room, or more house.

An' let me keep my one-room house,

Because the furniture I got don't fit in a two-room, three-room, four-room, or more house.

I like a one-room house.

Poet Alfred Kreymborg sued Durante for plagiarism. He maintained that Schnozzola's supposed original composition had been stolen from one of his verses and demanded $100,000 in damages. "If Mr. Durante is permitted to pilfer material without restraint," he told the court, "no poet is safe. Walt Whitman must be turning over in his grave."

"Walt Whiteman?" Jimmy said in a loud whisper to Jackson. "Wasn't he the district attorney in Gyp the Blood's case? Or maybe Paul's brother?"

The judge ruled in Durante's favor. "I strongly doubt that the defendant ever read a poem in his life," he said.

Apparently, Big Bill Duffy had smoked a peace pipe with the local bootleggers and was permitted to reopen his speakeasy. When *Show Girl* closed, Clayton, Jackson, and Durante resumed working at the Silver Slipper. They also accepted a lengthy engagement at the Palace. As if that weren't enough, they agreed to make a movie, *Roadhouse Nights*, in Paramount Picture's Astoria, Long Island, studio. It was about a gang of bootleggers whose hideout is a nightclub that caters to eccentric thugs and law enforcement officers.

The schedule was a tight one:

8:00 A.M. to 3:00 P.M.—Paramount's Long Island studio.
4:00 P.M. to 4:45 P.M.—Palace matinee.
8:00 P.M. to 9:50 P.M.—Silver Slipper.

10:05 P.M. to 10:50 P.M.—Palace theater's evening performance.
11:15 P.M. to 3:30 A.M.—Silver Slipper.

The script for *Roadhouse Nights* had been written by Ben Hecht and Charles MacArthur, two old friends from Club Durant days. For a month's work the trio was to receive $50,000. "How they got that sum is a delightful story," said Hecht, who enjoyed telling the story. It would get longer and funnier each time he related it:

"Jessie Lasky, the Paramount kingfish, summoned them to his spacious Astoria, Long Island, office. And with a great show of kindly generosity announced that out of the goodness of his heart he had decided to pay them $30,000. 'That's $10,000 for each of you men for working only a few hours a day for only three or four weeks,' Lasky said. Instead of being thanked as he had anticipated, Clayton, who was the spokesman for Durante and Jackson, refused the offer. Contemptuously he said, 'That's chicken feed to us!'

"Schnozzola squirmed when he heard his partner. 'But, Lou . . .' he started to say, 'No buts about it!' Clayton replied. 'We don't work for coolie wages. Fifty thousand! Nothing less!' Hearing this, Schnozzola slumped into his chair. Then he excused himself to go to the men's room. He was shaking so badly that he had to lean against the sink. About ten minutes later, Clayton walked in. 'Lou, I can't understand your attitude,' Durante said. 'I could use that money even if you can't. You ought to have accepted Lasky's offer.' Clayton calmly replied, 'How do you know that I didn't?' Then he showed Schnozzola a signed contract for $50,000. Jimmy was speechless. Suddenly, he began searching his partner's pockets. 'Why are you doing that?' Clayton asked. The almost hysterical Durante shouted, 'Lou, I want to find your loaded gun. You must have one that you held to Mr. Lasky's head!' "

Soon after completing *Roadhouse Nights*, the New York Stock Exchange collapsed. The get-rich-craze had appealed to almost everybody in the entertainment field, including the Durantes. At Jeanne's urging, they invested all their savings in the market. Their securities were now worthless. "Jimmy tried to be cool about it," said Jackson. " 'We got it a lot better than most folks,' he kept telling me. But despite his optimism, he was very upset. Each day he'd talk about stories he read in the newspapers. How homeless people had to sleep under bridges or on subways. By buying one drink a man could sleep on sawdust in a cheap speakeasy. He was really burned up when he read that one little girl was so hungry her mother fed her dog meal for supper. The story so moved him that he visited her and handed the family fifty dollars."

When Durante would get on the stage, his concern seemed to vanish. Instead, he'd start poking fun at the Depression. "Things are so bad," he'd say, "hotel clerks are now askin' guests if they want to rent the room for sleepin' or jumpin'?" Another frequent depression line was, "My friend, Groucho Marx, knows hard times are here because yesterday he saw pigeons in Central Park feedin' the people.' "

New York City's Mayor James J. Walker had recently told a group of Broadway theater owners that laughter was still the best medicine. That season more than a dozen shows were scheduled to open. The trio was featured in Cole Porter's *The New Yorkers*. It premiered at the Broadway Theater on December 8, 1930. This time the scenario called for them to be even zanier than they had been in *Show Girl*. They were cast as three unscrupulous but endearing screwballs who invade a Harlem speakeasy owned by a gun-shy gangster; they come to the aid of a love starved Park Avenue debutante; matriculate at a Sing Sing class in safecracking; attend a June garden wedding where the bridesmaids carry bouquets fashioned out of revolvers and switchblade knives.

Jimmy used the wood number at the end of the first act. Once again it received a tremendous response. One night while he was in the midst of extolling the virtues of lumber, the audience was startled when a small trained donkey revolted. The animal was supposed to listen patiently to Jimmy's spiel. During this performance it became bored, kicked Schnozzola, leaped off the stage, and wandered down the aisles. Durante didn't allow the incident to throw him. "Folks," he quickly said, "that animal is burnin' up because

91

the management refuses to give him a raise. Due to that unbearable situation, he's decided to quit. But let me talk person-to-person to that donkey an' maybe I can make him want to come back."

Then raising his voice several octaves, he said, "Listen kid, don't walk on me now. I promise that I'll pay you out of my own pocket. On my word of honor! So please come back. Remember, the show must go on!" The recalcitrant donkey seemed to understand Schnozzola, even if many humans didn't. When he trotted back peaceably, Jimmy added, "See my motto works: Never bite the hand that feeds you."

After 168 performances, *The New Yorkers* closed. Durante was promptly offered a five year Hollywood contract by Metro-Goldwyn-Mayer. Jimmy was to make three films a year at $35,000 each. "There's some kind of mistake," he said when he read it. "This thing says only my name."

Bartolomeo and Rosa Durante, Schnozzola's parents, emigrated from Salerno, Italy, in the 1880s. "New York streets not paved with gold," Bartolomeo once observed. "Only horse manure."

At the age of two Jimmy already had the ability to ham it up and make people feel sorry for him.

By the time Jimmy was twenty-one years old he had played ragtime in more than a dozen cabarets

Jimmy and his first wife, Jeanne, wearing matching knickers during a vacation in Clear Lake, California. "I put on hers by mistake," Schnozzola said. "It was a catostroke!"

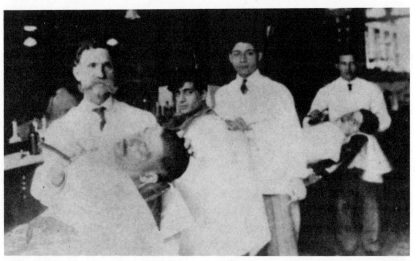

Most of the customers that patronized Bartolomeo's barbershop were Tammany Hall politicians.

Broadway's Three Sawdust Bums' motto was *Anything to make the audience laugh* (left to right: Lou Clayton, Durante, Eddie Jackson).

Durante appeared in a steady stream of second-rate movies. One of the slightly better films was *The Phantom President* in which he shared top honors with George M. Cohan.

In the mid-1930s, Jimmy made a "crook's tour" of Europe. "The city I liked best," he said, "is London. But they don't talk good like me."

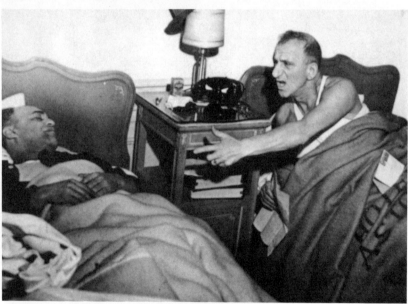

"Whenever I'm on the road," Jimmy explained in his usual preciseness, "me an' Eddie Jackson share a room because we both snore. That way we don't wake up each other."

The Broadway play *Red, Hot and Blue!*, starring Ethel Merman and Jimmy Durante, introduced newcomer Bob Hope. Between acts, Schnozzola and Hope compared noses.

Jimmy and Jeanne at the Santa Anita racetrack. Schnozzola's surefire betting system was to wager on every horse. "That way," he said shrewdly, "I'm guaranteed to win!"

Inset: During World War II, the U.S. Air Force reported that one of the most popular names for a plane was "Schnozzola."

Hollywood continued to assign Durante to movies that were doomed before they started. In 1938 he appeared in *Sally, Irene and Mary*. He played a sanitation man who had a phobia about picking up "dirty dirt."

Inset: Trick photography determined who had the bigger beak.

Schnozzola and Marlene Dietrich set records for the sale of World War II bonds. A government spokeswoman called them "America's secret weapon in the defeat of Hitler."

Inset: Jimmy and his father were always very close. "Maybe what I am today is because of him," Jimmy said. "Pop's the real comic in our family."

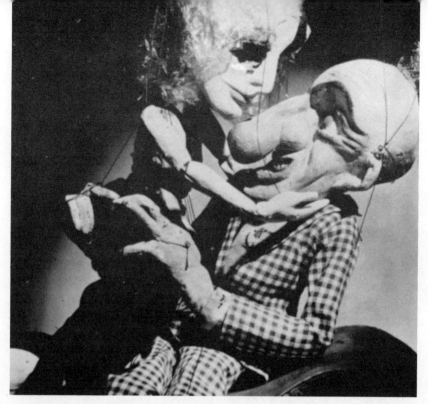

A Los Angeles museum featured marionettes that resembled famous movie stars. The chief attraction was a Greta Garbo doll sitting on the lap of a Schnozzola doll.

Jeanne Durante was frequently hospitalized. She died in 1943.

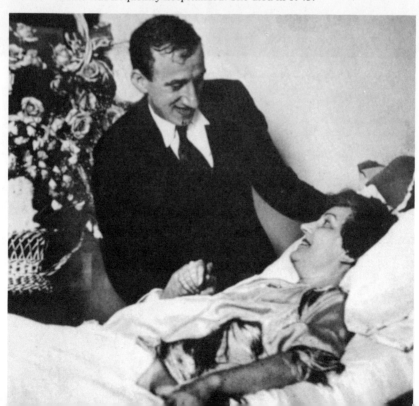

In the early forties, Schnozzola and Garry Moore cohosted a very successful radio show. Jimmy argued with guest Bing Crosby as to who could croon louder.

Opposite: In 1950, Jimmy switched to television. Opera star Helen Traubel was a frequent guest. "It's a pleasure to record with such a great artiste," she said. "One whose voice sounds the same with a broken needle."

Inset opposite: Next to poking fun at his nose, Jimmy drew the loudest laughs when he proclaimed himself as Broadway's best-dressed man.

Opposite: "Goodnight, Mrs. Calabash, wherever you are" was probably the best known sign-off in the history of radio and television.

Left: Seventeen years after his first wife's death, sixty-seven-year-old Jimmy Durante wed thirty-nine-year-old Margie Little.

Below: Shortly after their wedding, the Durantes adopted a week-old infant. "She's real nice," Schnozzola said. "But the poor kid got only a button for a nose!"

In 1935, Jimmy had appeared on Broadway in *Jumbo*. Nearly three decades later, MGM made it into a movie. Again, Schnozzola—and an elephant—were the star attractions.

Opposite: Durante's last movie was *It's a Mad, Mad, Mad, Mad World*. Although dozens of big-name comedians shared the spotlight, he was voted the film's outstanding funnyman.

Overleaf: "Goodnight, Jimmy, wherever you are" Bob Hope said at Jimmy's funeral. "But I'm sure it's the very center of heaven"

15

Hoity-toity Hollywood

MGM wanted only Jimmy Durante but he was reluctant to go solo. "You two guys have put up with me for years," he said to Clayton and Jackson. "We're a team an' nobody is goin' to split us for no amount of money!"

On June 28, 1931, he reluctantly signed the film contract when Clayton agreed to become his manager and Jackson his man Friday. "Each of you will get a third of everythin' I make," Jimmy said firmly. "An' that goes for as long as I live!"

Jeanne protested when she learned what her husband had promised. She had been ecstatic when the Hollywood offer was made and wanted to leave immediately. Now, she decided to stay in New York until their house was sold. Since Jimmy didn't enjoy traveling alone he was accompanied by his sister, her two sons, Jeanne's father, and Eddie Jackson. While waiting for the shooting to start he rented an ocean-front cottage for them in Venice, a Los Angeles suburb.

Clayton had left New York several days later because of pressing business—a giant crap game. The moment he arrived, the trio moved to a nearby hotel. A week later, during a heavy rainstorm, Jeanne appeared. Her car was loaded with presents, including a bright red smoking jacket she claimed was exactly like the one Ronald Colman had worn in a recent movie. Jeanne believed Colman was the most sophisticated actor she'd ever seen and tried desperately to get Jimmy to model himself after Colman. Schnozzola agreed to wear the smoking jacket. Somehow he "accidentally" stuffed it into a bundle of old clothes that was intended for the Salvation Army.

The movie continued to be delayed which allowed the Durantes a brief holiday in Clear Lake. "For six days I fished an' Jeannie cooked almost everythin' I caught," Jimmy said. "It was the best vacation the two of us ever had." Shortly after their return to Hollywood they were invited to a cocktail party at Pickfair, the legendary home of Mary Pickford and Douglas Fairbanks. The famous mansion was in sharp contrast to the tiny bungalow the Durantes had rented in Pasadena. On the ride home, Jeanne kept raving about Pickfair's elegance and enormous size. The following morning she did a complete about-face and claimed that Pickfair, like all of Hollywood, was too "hoity-toity" for her taste.

"Jeanne was like that," Jackson said. "She'd always blow hot and cold. Never lukewarm. Her Hollywood description again flip-flopped when Mary Pickford asked her to a tea she was giving for the French ambassador. As soon as Jeanne got back, Jimmy told me that she now had fresh ideas about Hollywood—all of them complimentary. She was so sold on the place that she began to nag him about buying a swanky car to match those the big stars rode around in. She wanted one like the Rolls Royce Fairbanks owned which had a bar and a portable toilet."

Despite the depression, Hollywood continued to glitter. Louis B. Mayer defended his stars' affluent ways. He had said, "They have to keep living that way so that the unemployed can plunk down their twenty-five cents admission charge and have renewed faith in the future."

When the filming of Jimmy's movie finally began, Jeanne often visited her husband on the MGM lot. He introduced her to Greta Garbo, Norma Shearer, John Barrymore, Wallace Beery, Marie Dressler, Robert Montgomery, and Joan Crawford. Crawford, who fancied herself as a gourmet chef, gave Jeanne a recipe for Boeuf à la Bourguignon. "That was a very nice thing for Joan to do," Jimmy said. "But why did I have to eat it five times a week?"

Durante's initial picture for MGM was *New Adventures of Get-Rich-Quick Wallingford*. William Haines, the film's star, was a passionate baseball fan. When he discovered that Jimmy shared his enthusiasm, he and Schnozzola formed a team. It was called "The Get-A-Run-Quick Niners." Robert Benchley, who had recently arrived in Hollywood for a movie assignment, watched one of the games. "Jimmy was the pitcher," he said, "Clayton, the catcher. I doubt if more conniving battery mates ever existed. Schnozzola would hide the ball in his uniform which was three sizes too large. Then he'd raise his foot and pretend he was tossing the ball. Clayton feigned to be bowled over by its tremendous speed. Eddie Jackson was the umpire. 'Strike!' he'd yell. When it came Jimmy's turn to bat, he'd fall to the ground as the ball whizzed by him. He'd claim the opposing pitcher was deliberately aiming at his nose. In a fury, Clayton rushed out to kill the offender. He was encouraged by the booing crowd. It seemed that the entire studio was on hand to cheer Schnozzola on. Even the high and mighty Louis B. Mayer, himself."

"I've got a poor head for names an' faces," Durante said. "So when this little guy in short sleeves an' a pencil hangin' on his ear says, 'Jimmy, you been workin' here for a couple of weeks an' never come to see me. Why don't you do it real soon?' I make him out for the cashier. 'That's very nice of you,' I tell him politely. 'I might need an advance at that. Who shall I ask for?' This little guy says, 'Louis B. Mayer. That's me.' Am I mortified!"

Eventually, Durante learned to recognize his employer. Several times, he, Clayton, Jackson, and Mayer ate lunch together in the studio commissary. On the way to their table they had to pass a large bird cage that contained three dice. The custom was that the low roller was required to pay the check. "Clayton was always high man," Jimmy said. "I'd be next. Then Jackson. Poor Mayer would rub my nose for luck, but always roll three snake eyes—a little three! Somehow

Clayton had learned to fix those dice. All the boss could do is scratch his head in shame."

"L. B. probably didn't mind losing," said Martin Liebermann, a MGM publicist. "He knew that Clayton was a close buddy of Durante. He wasn't taking any chances of upsetting them. After all, Schnozzola was a valuable property."

Mayer instructed Irving Thalberg, one of his top aides, to get Lloyds of London to underwrite Jimmy's nose for $1,000,000. A prime clause in the insurance contract stated that any accident which resulted in the nose being "abridged or beautified" would fetch immediate payment. Mayer got the publicity department to ballyhoo the transaction.

A writer from *Photoplay* magazine asked Durante if the nose promotion had made him self-conscious? "I guess without my proboscitor I'd be just another moral," Jimmy said. "But I got to admit that it has some pullbacks. Like the time I had a blind date with a girl who didn't know me. I talked to her on the telephone. 'Hello,' I say. An' she says, 'You sound like you got a nice voice. Come right over.' So I rush over to her house. When I get there she takes one look at my nose an' says, 'You must have come in such a hurry that you forget to hang up the telephone.' Little did that girl know I'd become a dashin' movie star."

Durante's next film was *The Cuban Love Song* starring Lawrence Tibbett. When Jeanne learned that the famous singer was going to be in the movie, she told Jimmy for the hundredth time, "He's the one who said my voice was outstanding. We're old friends."

After spending two hours in the beauty parlor and purchasing an expensive dress, she went to the MGM lot to see him. It was obvious that Tibbett failed to remember her. When she recalled their last meeting, he told her that she had been wise in marrying Jimmy and leaving show business behind. Jeanne was so angry that she stamped out and refused to speak to her husband for days.

Although MGM liked to stress they were "The Home of Family Values," the titles of their movies suggested the opposite. *The Cuban Love Song*, like Jimmy's following films for MGM, were critical as well as box office failures. In *The Passionate Plumber* he played second fiddle to a fading Buster Keaton. *The Wet Parade* required him to twitch his nose, roll his eyes, and say, "Hot-cha-cha" several times. *Speak Easily* was another Buster Keaton supposed-comedy. Shooting for that movie was often delayed because of Keaton's drinking problem. He was having marital trouble and would disappear for days. When the picture was finally completed, he and Jimmy were requested to attend a special press conference. Durante showed. Keaton didn't. Schnozzola tried to protect his absent co-star by saying his nonattendance had been caused by a bad cold. The cover-up attempt didn't work.*

The next day Keaton received a telegram from the studio informing him that his services were no longer required. Jimmy talked to Mayer and after an hour of intense pleading he managed to get Buster reinstated. His reward was to be teamed with Keaton in another disastrous movie, *What! No Beer?* Bernard Sobel, a columnist for the New York *American,* said, "Durante got more laughs than Keaton, but that wasn't very much."†

Between takes, Jimmy was frequently asked by other actors to perform routines from his old nightclub act. He obliged. One of the most appreciative spectators was Greta Garbo, who was making a movie on the adjoining set. At the time this occurred, a local museum was arranging a marionette exhibition. A doll resembling Garbo was the featured attraction. When a museum curator learned about her interest in Durante, the Garbo doll was placed on the lap of the Schnozzola marionette. A reporter asked the Swedish film star for a comment. The normally taciturn actress, who often went to absurd lengths to avoid the press, seemed pleased to reply. "I don't mind this," she said. "Mr. Schnozzola is a dear man. I admire him a lot." Clayton posted a clipping of the

---

*Keaton's absence was compounded when, at the time of the MGM meeting, he was involved in a drunken barroom brawl. A photograph of the incident appeared in the morning newspapers.

† The studio felt *What! No Beer?* was so bad they held back its release for more than a year. This happened to several of Durante's films.

story on the wall of Jimmy's dressing room. Jeanne saw it and tore it down.

In the fall of 1932, Jimmy was loaned to Paramount to co-star with George M. Cohan in *The Phantom President*. The film satirized a traveling medicine man who is mistaken for a presidential candidate. Schnozzola was to play Cohan's unlettered but shrewd political advisor. Cohan, the idol of Broadway, was reluctant to go to Hollywood. As a favor to Durante whom he knew from vaudeville days, he agreed to make the movie. "I want to see my old pal get a decent break," he said. "Jimmy Durante has that special quality that reaches the heart as well as the funny bone."

While *The Phantom President* was in production, the Durantes moved to a large apartment in northern Los Angeles. They invited Cohan and Jackson to dinner. Jeanne prepared the recipe Joan Crawford had given her. "I guess it was cooked too long," said Jackson. "What came out was rubbery. Cohan said something about it that Jeanne took as an insult. With that she marched out and shut herself up in the bedroom. No amount of coaxing could get her out. Cohan was embarrassed, but not nearly as much as Jimmy. I'd never seen him so angry. He decided on a trial separation—it lasted two whole days!"

The critics were a little kinder to *The Phantom President*. "It's not the best," wrote Bernard Sobel. "But at least Schnozzola is allowed to display some of his Broadway talent.... Wonder of wonder, he is allowed to say more than hot-cha-cha." Sobel singled out one of Jimmy's lines: "A Depression is a hole, a hole is nothin', an' why should I waste my time talkin' about nothin'." That remark became very popular. It was repeated by President Roosevelt in one of his Fireside Chats.

Mayer personally welcomed Durante back to MGM. "From now on things will be different," he promised. "I guarantee you'll only be put in the cream of the crop." He quickly forgot and tossed Schnozzola into *Hell Below*, a formula submarine B-movie that was being shot in Hawaii. Jimmy was the ship's cook. In addition to feeding the crew, he was required to box a kangaroo. The dialogue included such gems as, "It may be darn close in here but us sub guys are real men. So sissies better keep out!" Near the ending, Jimmy said, "We may wind up in the deep six but we'll have died for the cause of liberty. But if you don't mind, hand me a life preserver." His next films were no better. The studio was doing very little to help the comedian's sinking career.

He was grateful when in February of 1933, he was asked to star in *Strike Me Pink*, a new Broadway musical that was having a casting problem. Waxy Gordon, a bootleg potentate, was the show's chief financial backer. A play doctor had told him that if *Strike Me Pink* was to survive, a name comic was essential. To save his investment, Waxy sent an SOS to Schnozzola. Jimmy got a leave of absence from MGM and promptly went into rehearsal.

The play got off to a jolly start. At the beginning of the first act a spotlight focused on Jimmy standing in the aisle. He was arguing with an usher who refused him entrance to the stage. "But I'm in the cask," Schnozzola protested. His exasperation increased when an imposter had the gall to tell the audience that he was the real Jimmy Durante.

"I guess maybe he's me an' maybe I'm not who I think I am," Schnozzola said dejectedly as he turned to leave. At which point the fake Durante revealed his true identity. A relieved Schnozzola was allowed to join the "cask." For the next two and half hours the audience roared. Especially at the finale, a six-day bicycle race skit. Jimmy was so exuberant that occasionally he rode his bike into the orchestra pit. No one was hurt but the frightened musicians made him sign an affidavit that he'd be more careful in the future. Jimmy responded to curtain calls by singing to the tune of "Wintergreen for President"—"Roosevelt is President." It never failed to bring the audience to its feet in a roaring ovation. After 105 performances, *Strike Me Pink* closed. It meant Durante returning to Hollywood to make some more lemons.

More Screen Disasters

Most of these films wound up as being the lower half of double feature programs. They included:

Palooka

In that movie, Durante was the manager of a dim-witted pugilist who adored flowers. "That's okay with me," Schnozzola said. "As long as I don't have to pick him up from smellin' the daisies." There were a great many similar lines in this stereotyped script. The movie's salvation came when Jimmy introduced "Inka Dinka Doo," which later became his theme song. He constantly changed the words. One of his early unpublished versions was:

> Say it with roses,
> Say it with furs,
> Say it with Rolls Royces,
> Say it with purrs,
> Say it with diamonds,
> Say it with drink,
> But always be careful not to say it with ink
> A-dink-a-dinka, dink-a-doo.

Hollywood Party

Tarzan of the jungle was very popular at the time. In a parody of the ape man, Schnozzola—named Scharzan—beat his chest and yelled "hot-cha-cha" as he battled a lion. Lupe Velez was cast as Scharzan's Jane. The jungle was filled with wild beasts but she knew that her hero would protect her. "Save me! Save me!" she shouted.

"I'm not Scharzan the Shoutin' Conquerer for nothin'," he replied. One of the few people to laud *Hollywood Party* was Jeanne Durante, who had a walk-on role in the film. Jackson said that she went to see herself at least half a dozen times.

Student Tour

Jimmy was chaperon to a group of prankish coeds and athletes who were on a world cruise. He constantly had to stop his charges from playfully cutting each other's ties, administering hotfoot tricks, and tossing unsuspecting victims into the ship's swimming pool. Lucille Ball played a nurse in that movie. "Not even Schnozzola could save the dreadful picture," she said. "It wasn't a B-movie or even a C. But a Y——Y for yecchy!"

Musicals are often weak in plot. "This one was completely debilitated," said Lucille Ball. With mock dismay Jimmy observed Rudy Vallee kissing Alice Faye; Faye pursuing Vallee; Vallee allowing himself to be pursued; Vallee pursuing Faye. At the conclusion they kissed as Durante engaged in a conversation with a quacking wooden duck. However, all was not lost. The film did give Jimmy's fans an opportunity to see him perform in blackface.

While Durante was making these flops, Will H. Hays, who had formerly served as Postmaster General under President Harding, now headed the Motion Picture Producers and Distributers of America. This new organization, a self-censoring body whose goal was to send out inoffensive, morally uplifting films, did its job so successfully that Hollywood soon acquired a reputation throughout the world for displaying an unrealistic view of life. Hays was a close friend of William Randolph Hearst. The newspaper magnet vigorously approved his code which included the following don'ts:

- Use of profanity. (Words like *damn, S.O.B.,* and *hell* were erased.)
- So was "lengthy" kissing and "lustful" embracing.
- Scenes of childbirth.
- Miscegenation.
- White slavery.
- Ministers were never to be portrayed as villains or comic characters.

Anything regarded as being salacious was quickly eliminated. Hays felt that one of Durante's songs had sexual innuendos. He insisted that it be removed. Clayton was indignant. He stormed into Hay's office and demanded an apology. "The man doesn't have an obscene bone in his body," he shouted. It was one of the few times Hays rescinded an order. He allowed the song to remain in.

Clayton may have been exaggerating slightly. Jimmy was responsible for some suggestive statements, but rarely while performing. Michael Mok, a reporter for the New York *Post*, was walking along Broadway with Schnozzola when they noticed an extremely tiny man wearing a feather in his hatband. At his side was a very tall, very stout woman. Durante stared at the oddly matched couple. Then he whispered to Mok, "Look! Look! A mountain climber!"

Jimmy managed to squeeze in an appearance at the El Roco, a posh Washington, D.C., cabaret, while he was making these films. One night, General Hugh Johnson, who was the director of President Roosevelt's NRA (National Recovery Administration), was in the audience. His secretary had announced a week before that he'd be there. Schnozzola welcomed his guest with a song he had especially composed for the occasion. He called it "The Alphabet Stew":

> The NRA, CCC, WPA an' AAA,
> The PWA, FWP, CWA an' TVA.

New letters every single day.
Hey FDR, how about a FFE?

When Johnson asked him what FFE stood for, Jimmy replied, "Phones for Everybody. The TVA gave electric lights to everybody who didn't have any. So now phones. Fair's fair."*

Many of Durante's movies were disappointing because the film industry refused to allow him to come out with his own brand of comedy. Invariably, studio bigwigs erased some of his funniest material.

A sketch in the movie *Hollywood Party* was scrapped because it was felt the audience would dismiss it as slapstick comedy and fail to find it amusing. Jimmy (Scharzan) is sitting serenely in a tree crooning to his mate, Lupe Velez. He is startled when a coconut lands on his nose. He brushes it off. A moment later the same thing happens. Patiently, he removes the coconut. When it occurs the third time he becomes indignant. "Go ahead," he ad-libbed. "Touch that nose just once more an' I'll sue this jungle for every dollar you got. I'll turn this here joint into a bowlin' alley!" Another sketch the cinema audience didn't get to see was when Jimmy picked up a fallen branch and suddenly started beating the trees. "Why are you doing that?" Velez asks. "To wake up all the birds," Jimmy replies. "When Scharzan don't sleep, nobody sleeps!"

In *Student Tour* one of removed sequences showed Jimmy relaxing at the beach. He peacefully ignored the flies that swarmed all over him. However, when one landed on his nose, he angrily tossed down his sun visor and yelled, "Just for that bit of misbehavin', you all have to get off!" The cameramen were so busy laughing they forgot to reload and the scene had to be done over. They laughed even harder the second time. Yet, the completed scene was cut.

"The studio felt that movie audiences just wouldn't get his style of jokes," Jackson said. "And with the Depression going

---

*Trying to stem the Depression, President Roosevelt established a series of New Deal agencies: CCC—Civilian Conservation Corps, WPA—Works Progress Administration, AAA—Agricultural Adjustment Administration, PWA—Public Works Administration, FWP—Federal Writer's Project, CWA—Civil Works Administration, TVA—Tennessee Valley Administration.

on they weren't taking any chances. Besides, at first, Jimmy didn't complain—he was too busy house hunting. The minute he got through shooting, Jeanne would drag him to look at a house she wanted to buy. Most of them ran into the heavy thousands. You'd think she was some kind of heiress the way she went about it. It was one of the few times I ever heard Jimmy say no to her."

During the filming of *Hollywood Party* the Durantes bought a small stucco house near the MGM studio. Although it stood on a 85-by-150 foot plot, Jeanne pretentiously named it "The Dural Farm." While she and Jimmy were both away a burglar broke in. Among the items taken was a music box that had been a wedding present from Jimmy's father. A large reward was offered with no questions asked. It wasn't recovered. Several months later, Durante received a letter from San Quentin Prison:

"Dear Schnozzola,

I've been meaning to write to you for a long time to tell you where your music box can be found. I turned it over to the sheriff's office and I've written to him to say that it is yours. I'm so ashamed, Jimmy, I'll take no reward from you. I had no idea that it was your house when I broke in or I never would have done it. And the boys up here would never speak to me if they knew I'd stolen something from their greatest pal."

Durante was delighted to learn the whereabouts of the music box. As soon as it was retrieved he and the convict began exchanging letters and Christmas cards. He showed Bob Hope a hand-painted card his penitentiary pen pal had sent him. "That was Schnozzola's strong belief," Hope said. "Many times he insisted that given a decent break no man is a sinner. Except maybe a studio boss."

When Clayton complained to Mayer that Jimmy's popularity was slipping because of all the B-movies, he was told that what Durante needed was a public buildup. Mayer suggested that Schnozzola make a personal tour in major cities. "Jimmy did," said Jackson. "He visited about a dozen theaters that MGM owned or controlled. As soon as the curtain went up, Jimmy would hop off the stage and mingle with the audience. At one matinee in Pittsburgh, he kissed the cheek of a lady sitting in an aisle seat. When he got back to the stage he said, 'Boy, I can't forget that gal.' The lady laughed and started applauding. But the next day we heard that she was suing Jimmy for five thousand dollars. She said that he had humiliated her in front of friends."

While a lawyer was working out an out-of-court settlement, Jimmy moped in his hotel suite. "Jeanne hadn't come with him," Jackson said. "But the radio reported what happened and she must have thought Jimmy was playing around. She kept calling him up."

Jackson remembered his muttering, "I'm innocent. There was no evil content in my actions!"

To help cheer him up, Jackson and Clayton decided on playing a practical joke. They secured the services of an unemployed actor who often portrayed a priest. They coached him on what he was supposed to tell Durante. They were both present when early the next morning there was a knock on Jimmy's hotel room door. Still wearing a bathrobe he answered it.

"I'm Father Zybyzko of St. Mary's Church," said the visitor who was dressed in clerical clothing.

"Come in, Father," Jimmy said. "Make yourself comfortable on the stuffed couch. What can I do for you so early in the mornin'?"

"We want to build a new parochial school and you can help. We want you to perform at our church. Unless you're one of those lazy bums that never goes to church."

"I never miss goin' to church regularly. Why I have a ring that a Cardinal gave me. See?"

"Stop interrupting me when I'm talking. Think you're better than me because you got a ring!"

"I didn't mean no harm, Father. To show what I mean, let me give you a check for $100 for all the good work you're doin'."

"Think you can bribe me with your check. I heard about you show business bigots!"

"Father, I swear I didn't mean no harm. The check was only to show my appreciation."

"Look, you big bum, I don't need your charity!"

At this point Jackson couldn't stand the masquerade any longer. "It's all a gag," he admitted. "This guy isn't a real priest. We promised him a sawbuck if he could fool you."

For a moment, Schnozzola appeared to be annoyed by the deception. Then he joined in the laughter as the bogus priest removed his turned collar. "For such good fakin'," Jimmy said. "This guy deserves at least double what you promised." He reached for his wallet and handed the fake clergyman a fifty dollar bill. "Put some of that in the church poor box," he said. "Maybe that way your sin will be blotted out."

Money rarely concerned Jimmy. He was known for his generosity. "Panhandlers would wait for him at the MGM entrance," Jackson said. "That was one of the reasons for Jeanne's displeasure. She'd lecture him about his easy come, easy go feelings about money. To please her, Jimmy would promise that he would stop. But by the next week he'd be back to his normal self—a soft touch."

In the autumn of 1933, the Chase and Sanborn coffee company offered to pay him $5,000 a week to host their Sunday night radio program. MGM gave him permission. That sum was in addition to what he was earning as a Hollywood actor. It put his yearly income in excess of a quarter of a million dollars. Jeanne and Jackson went along with him for the Chase and Sanborn signing. Clayton was in New York at the time.*

Deprived of Clayton's judicious guidance, Schnozzola said, "That's a lot of money you're payin' me. Are you sure you want to do it?" His wife tried to silence him by kicking his foot. She did it so forcefully that he toppled over and tore his jacket. Dusting himself off, he told the startled executives, "Better add $19.95 to the first check you give me so I can buy myself a new suit."

---

*Not for a crap game, but participating in a giant billiard match.

17

"What Elephant?"

Possessing a lucrative MGM contract would have satisfied most performers. Not Durante. He was tired of appearing in so many second-rate movies. Being host of a radio program that catered to "smart axes" didn't appeal to him either. He pleaded with Clayton to find him a Broadway vehicle. "Lou, I'll settle for bein' second banana or even third." Clayton told him to be patient and wait for the right one.

"Jimmy waited," said Jackson. "At times not so patiently. Not that he was a nagger, but it got to the point where he'd keep at Lou with all his might. And besides, Jeanne wasn't much help—she was in one of her no-talking periods."

To get his mind off his unhappiness, Durante agreed to give a series of six lectures at a UCLA drama class. His topic was, "The Significance of Comedy." Loretta Lambert, a former bit player, was one of the students. "I was in films with Tallulah Bankhead and Charles Boyer," she said proudly. "I must admit that when I first heard that Schnozzola was going to speak to us, I had strong reservations. In those days I thought of myself as strictly a very serious actress, one who frowned on the asinine shenanigans of someone like Durante. That's the way I pigeonholed him—a buffoon clown from the toss-a-pie-in-your-face school. What could he teach me?"

Although Loretta Lambert kept repeating that her memory was no longer dependable, she seemed to have total recall. "Durante was often accompanied by one of his friends named Clayton who was always reminding him of the good old days," she said. "Each time he did, a wonderful smile would appear on Schnozzola's face as he relived the past. However, he never boasted about himself. Actually the reverse. Someone else was always the main attraction. Quite a change from Basil Rathbone, who had been our last guest lecturer. The way Rathbone related an incident in his clipped British accent, he'd sound as if he personally had been responsible for making the sun come up!

"But don't think that humility was Schnozzola's sole attribute. He taught us that no matter what role you were assigned to, it was quite necessary to realize that the audience is never fooled—they can always tell when an actor is faking. 'Love them,' Durante would say, 'and they will love you back. It's the way you deliver your lines that counts. That's a lot more important then what's in them.' He'd demonstrate by peeling off joke after joke. Many of them were stale and overworked. But the technique he used made those jokes come alive."

When Jimmy completed his final UCLA lecture in October 1934, Billy Rose, a prominent Broadway producer, announced that he was about to stage "The most stupendous extravaganza ever to hit the Great White Way." The play, *Jumbo*, had outstanding credentials: book by Ben Hecht and Charles MacArthur; songs by Richard Rodgers and Larry Hart; directed by George Abbott; staged by John Murray Anderson.

Since Durante's movie contract called for a two month vacation, he headed East for an audition. Rose instantly selected him for one of the leads. He agreed to pay Schnozzola $3,000 a week to play Claudius Brainy Bowers, a trumpet-tongued press agent for an ailing one-ring circus that was on the verge of bankruptcy. "Right away I knew that *Jumbo* was for me," Jimmy said. "It had wonderment for old people, their married children, an' even their grandchildren. Every single critic felt just like me. They couldn't stop ravin'. Also that show was filled with lots of hauntin' songs."*

In the first act Durante was required to offer the owner of the circus some free advice on how to attract much-needed customers. He suggested, "Put twelve acrobats up there, hangin' by their toes. Fill the ring with elephants, lions, tigers, an' kangaroos; I'll even let you throw in a penguin. Then have a beautiful voluptuous woman. Do what I tell you an' you'll have the greatest show this side of oblivion."

Before his recommendations could be adopted, the bank attached the circus's only asset, a giant elephant named Big Rosie alias Jumbo. Schnozzola, who had gotten very fond of Jumbo, attempted to hide her from the law. That scene provided Jimmy with one of the funniest lines ever delivered in the theater. Attempting to smuggle Jumbo past a roadblock, Durante was halted by the sheriff while leading the tremendous beast.

"Where are you going with that elephant?" the lawman asked.

"What elephant?" Jimmy replied innocently as he tried to dodge a loving pat from the animal's trunk.

The sheriff insisted that it was Jumbo. "I know when someone is trying to fool me," he said.

"Honest, this is Rosie, my own private household pack-adermite," Jimmy said. "Rosie always wants to play. Don't you Rosie? Let's show the nice man." To remove any doubt, Jimmy stretched out on the ground. The elephant promptly lifted up her huge right forefoot over Schnozzola's head and held it there for ten seconds. "See!" Jimmy said triumphantly. "That proves she is my personal household pet."

Frank Buck, a big game hunter known as "Bring 'Em Back Alive," later told Durante that he wouldn't attempt that trick for a million dollars. But for 223 performances Schnozzola put his trust in the elephant. After the show closed, Big Rosie was retired to an animal farm. Jimmy paid the elephant a

---

*"The Most Beautiful Girl in the World," "Little Girl Blue," "Over and Over," "Song of the Roustabouts," "My Romance."

visit. The moment he saw her he yelled, "Rosie! Rosie! It's Nosey!" She trumpeted; and then as if responding to cue, nudged him to the ground exactly the way she used to do in the act. Durante was overjoyed. "Rosie remembers me," he shouted. "She still loves me."

Without consulting him, Clayton hadn't renewed Jimmy's MGM contract. Instead, late in 1935, he arranged for an overseas tour. For a thousand pounds a week—approximately $5,000—Schnozzola was to perform abroad. When Jeanne learned about the intended trip, she blew her top. She protested so violently that Jimmy decided not to go. Instead, he accompanied her back to California. From past experience Clayton held off canceling the tour. Sure enough, Jeanne soon changed her mind. A few days after they arrived on the West Coast she told Jimmy that traveling to the continent would be broadening for them—Mary Pickford and Joan Crawford did it constantly.

The Durantes packed their suitcases and took the Santa Fe Chief to New York. In Manhattan they planned to board the *S.S. Normandie*, which was making its first West to East crossing. However, when the train made a brief stop in Pasadena, Jeanne did a flip-flop and had the porter remove her luggage. Jimmy tried to reason with her, but she was adamant. He continued on alone. By the time he reached New York he decided that his place was at the side of his wife. "Lou, I'm not goin' to Europe," he told Clayton. "It's crazy for me to leave Jeannie all by herself. An' that's final!"

A few minutes later Jimmy telephoned his wife to announce the news. Rather than being pleased with his decision, she pointed out that he was slipping and badly needed the international exposure. "You'll only be gone for six weeks," she said. "During that time I plan to stay with my mother. So you needn't worry about me."

"But he was worried," said Billy Rose, who was aware of the situation. "Jimmy had good reason to be. What followed next was unbelievable. If I dared to include the episode in one of my shows, the audience would rebel. Mrs. Durante's back-and-forth tennis routine had poor Schnozzola baffled. Despite her assurance that she wanted him to go abroad, he felt that he best return to Los Angeles. But wily Lou Clayton had other ideas. Bigheartedly, he offered to secure Jimmy's train ticket and check his suitcases. Instead, he sent them to Schnozzola's cabin aboard the *Normandie*. Then he said that since Jimmy had a great deal of time before the train's departure, they should make an appearance at a bon voyage party that was being given for Ben Goetz, an MGM executive. There were a great many guests present—I was among them. We had all been tipped off about Clayton's shanghai plan.

"There was a piano in Goetz' cabin and Jimmy entertained us. While he was playing and clowning, the guests slipped away one by one. The only people remaining were Goetz, Durante, Clayton, and myself—I had to make a business trip to London. Jimmy was so busy pounding the piano and singing he didn't pay any attention to the 'All ashore' warnings or to any of the ship's blasts. Suddenly, he yelled, 'We're movin'!' Clayton tried to reassure him. 'Don't worry,' he said. 'We can get off on 125th Street.' But Schnozzola wasn't buying it. 'What do you think this is?' he shouted. 'The night boat to Albany? Lou, you tricked me an' I don't even know the language they speak over there!' "

London Loves Sir Schnozzola

Jimmy was surprised to learn that his films were widely distributed in Great Britain and that he was considered one of the leading "Yank comics." When his ship docked, he was greeted by dozens of admiring English movie buffs. A giggling, scarecrowish dental assistant, who identified herself as president of the Schnozzola Fan Club of the United Kingdom, presented him with a huge carrot cake shaped in the form of a nose. A representative from Lloyds of London carefully scrutinized the crowd. When asked what he was doing, he replied that he was making certain that nothing happened to Durante's highly insured "olfactory organ." Clayton quickly arranged a press conference where most of the questions revolved around Jimmy's nose:

- How did he manage to get close enough to do any kissing?
- Did his nose present any shaving problems?
- Was it affected by high altitudes?
- Could it sniff out rainy or foggy days?

The next day many of the English newspapers ran feature stories about Schnozzola's nose. It was compared to an immense rubber cigar, a snow plow, the handle of a giant paint brush, a banana that forgot to stop growing, and a gigantic sausage that could provide nourishment for dozens of starving people. The high-hatted writer of the sedate London *Times* wrote: "It is indeed a remarkable nose which differentiates itself from other remarkable noses. It may not have the tremendous hook of Lord Chatham's, nor wildly ambitious like Lady Hester Stanhope's, nor grandly aquiline like the Iron Duke's, but as one studies it closely there is a temptation to think it must be prehensile, like an elephant's trunk."

Durante was a sensation in Blackpool and Liverpool. Audiences hailed his talent. At one performance he was required to take so many curtain calls that even though all the lights were turned off the crowd refused to leave. The manager was forced to come on stage and plead for people to go home. A compromise was finally reached when they agree to depart if Schnozzola sang one more chorus of "Inka Dinka Doo."

In Glasgow, Clayton told him that Sir Harry Lauder, the great Scottish comedian, was sitting in a front row. In a hoarse stage whisper that could clearly be heard in the back of the house, Jimmy confided that he used to save his barbershop tips to see Lauder perform in New York. Sir Harry was so moved that he ran up to the stage where he began clowning with Schnozzola. He tried to teach him to recite a favorite local rhyme which Lauder had set to song. It was "The Wee Hoose 'Mang the Heather." When he finished, a querulous looking Durante said, "I don't speak Scotch so good, translate it for me." After several minutes of intense coaching, Jimmy felt that he had mastered it:

> There's a weepin' house in the water
> That needs fixin' up for a weepin' lassie.
> If you saw her, you'd weep too.
> Just the same as me.

There was thunderous applause when Jimmy finished. A delighted Sir Harry Lauder said, "Now, I see why your countrymen regard you so highly." A few days later Durante's appearance at London's Palladium Music Hall was equally successful—for two weeks he played to capacity audiences. He was the highest priced entertainer ever to perform there. A press representative of the Palladium, England's leading vaudeville house, said, "During that week I was the most sought-after bloke in town. Everybody wanted a ticket including members and future members of the royal family.* We had billed him as 'Jimmy Schnozzola Durante, the Hollywood Lover.' It's a huge mistake to label Britishers as being dispassionate. This audience was beside itself. From the turbulent reception he received he could have been knighted Sir Schnozzola."

Durante was intrigued by London's pagentry. Afternoons when he wasn't giving a matinee, he could usually be found at Buckingham Palace watching the changing of the guard. However, he demonstrated his allegiance to commoners by being made an honorary cockney† and adopting some of their rhyming slang. For weeks he went around saying, "Don't knock my 'I suppose' (nose). Or telling waiters, "Give me the 'goose's neck' (check)."

While in London he visited Eton, one of England's most prestigious public schools. He was impressed by the big Eton collars and short, black jackets the smaller boys wore and also the butterfly ties and morning coats the older students paraded around in. When he learned that Eton teachers were called beaks, he remarked, "With this beak of mine I ought to become the principal of this place!" Durante was upset when he noticed that students and teachers raised their index fingers the instant they passed each other on the street. "That ain't a nice thing to do," Jimmy said. He knew that Italians often used finger gestures to indicate displeasure. Later, he was relieved when he learned that in Eton the finger greeting was a hallowed tradition.

*   *   *

*Young Philip, Mountbatten, now husband of Queen Elizabeth, was in the audience. Referring to Durante, he said, "American hilarity at its best. A bit madcap but delicious."

† Londoners born within the sound of Bow Bells (St. Mary-le-Bow Church).

Several times a week Jimmy placed an overseas telephone call to his wife. Most of the conversations were long-winded as she gave him a complete rundown of her daily routine—little was excluded. He learned that Jeanne's mother had ordered a new kitchen table from the Montgomery Ward catalogue, and that she'd eaten a strawberry frappé that had given her a bellyache. Most of the calls ended with, "Hurry home, Tootis. I miss you terribly."

Schnozzola discovered that he was not going back to the States as soon as he thought. London's Denham Studio wanted him to appear in a British-made movie, *Land Without Music*. He was to receive forty thousand American dollars for a month's filming. Another trans-Atlantic phone call was made. Jimmy expected his wife to be very upset when she learned about the new delay. She wasn't. "Since you're thousands of miles away," she said, "you might as well make the most out of it. Don't hurry home on my account. I'm doing fine."

Before the British motion picture was scheduled to begin production, Clayton arranged for Jimmy to give ten performances in Dublin's Theater Royal. After the first show, Durante noticed a large group of youngsters lined up outside the stage door. When they spotted him, they set up a chant, "We want Schnozzola! We want Schnozzola!" Those on bicycles followed his taxi to the Gresham Hotel where he was staying. The next day he arranged a special matinee where children were admitted free.

Between performances Durante was visited by members of the famous Abbey Players. He joined them in discussing the various forms of acting. It was apparent their accent troubled him. The moment they left he turned to Clayton and asked suspiciously, "Was they praisin' or knockin' me?" He was comforted when one of them traveled to England to observe him film *Land Without Music*.

Unfortunately, the script for the movie wasn't very good. Hedda Hopper described *Land Without Music* as an "English-bred turkey without any lean meat, only gobs of feckless fat ... a butcher's sharp knife is needed to put it out of its misery." The gossip columnist was well-known for her inaccuracy. This time she had described the movie correctly. *Land Without Music* was truly an "English-bred turkey." The plot was silly: Princess Regent, ruler of the Duchy of Lucco, issued a proclamation forbidding all forms of music. Jimmy was cast as an American newspaperman who restored laughter and song to that unhappy land. "I'll do anythin' so everybody gets a fair chance to sing," Jimmy said at the beginning of the film. His "anythin' " was often quite ludicrous.

During the making of *Land Without Music*, Durante was taken to the exclusive Garrick Club. Afterwards he talked about his experience to Quentin Reynolds who was staying at the same hotel. "It was so classy that everybody had to wear a black umbrella an' a black bowler hat an' a black striped suit," he said. "No monkey business was allowed. Why, a member got himself kicked out for cheatin' in Whist. That's a card playin' game. An' another one for pinchin' a servant lady in a personal place. There's even a special smokin' room where the members hold cigars an' blow smoke rings in shapes of pound money."

When the movie was completed, Jimmy decided to make a "crook's" tour of the Continent. "Jeannie thinks I'll get culture by visitin' places like Paris an' Rome," he told Clayton who had to return immediately so that he could arrange for Durante to appear in a Broadway play, *Red, Hot and Blue!* Schnozzola set out alone.

Two weeks went by without any word of his whereabouts. Scotland Yard, *la Sûreté*, and Interpol were alerted. He was finally located in Salerno, Italy. "I figured while I was doin' so much travelin'," he said, "I should see the place where my mother an' father was born in. I still got lots of relatives there who look just like me. They made me feel so good that I get neuralgic when I think of that place."

19

Top Billing

Two passengers aboard the *S.S. Conte di Savoia*—Jimmy Durante and Victoria Eugenia, former Queen of Spain—had cocktails together on their last night at sea. Reporters met them both when the ship reached Manhattan. At a joint press conference Schnozzola patted the Queen's head as he said, "This here lady once had a real crown but she's not even stuck-up. She's very smart an' knows a lot. For instance she told me all about Napoleon an how tickled to death he is when he gets back from Elbow. Maybe she talks fancy, but she's just like a regular human bein'."

Victoria Eugenia smiled appreciatively. "Mr. Durante was an excellent traveling companion," she said. "He made the trip most enjoyable. But who are Razor Riley and Pretty Boy Moran he kept talking about?"

Jimmy went directly from the pier to Broadway's Alvin Theater to start rehearsals for Cole Porter's new musical, *Red, Hot and Blue!* His co-star was the back-row belting singer Ethel Merman. The cast also included a fast-rising young comedian named Bob Hope. "It was my first major role," Hope said. "I guess that I was scared. Each time I showed it,

117

Jimmy would put me at ease. 'Don't you worry, kid,' he'd say. 'My schnozzle is even funnier than yours.' "

Merman demanded that she get top billing because hers was the more prominent name. Durante was willing to give it to her, but Jeanne, who had just arrived from California, objected. Vinton Freedly, the show's producer, came up with a solution—a railroad crossing type of presentation:

The script for *Red, Hot and Blue!* was complicated. Bertram "Policy" Pinkle (Durante), a left-handed confidence man who had once captained a prison polo team, was asked for help by Nails O'Reilly (Merman), a former manicurist who became a wealthy widow when her gangster husband met his end. She hoped to gain admission to high society by conducting a lottery for charity. The idea for the dignified raffle was the brainchild of lawyer Bob Hope. He was in love with Nails but couldn't express his true feelings because it would mean revealing the name of a young woman who had sat on a waffle iron when she was four-years-old.

The involved show was filled with lots of pumpkin-headed gags, but Jimmy's constant-changing expressions saved them.

Durante: You know what Aristole said about the legal mind?
Merman: No.
Durante: That makes us even.

Durante: Loan me five thousand dollars.
Hope: Do you think I am a millionaire?

Durante: Well then make it five dollars!

Durante: Please don't cry. Don't be lugubrious.
Merman: What does lugubrious mean?
Durante: Go ahead an' cry.

For some unknown reason Jimmy was costumed in George Washington garb and identified himself as the Valley Forger. In the third act he had to appear before a Senate investigating committee. Serving as his own lawyer he dashed back and forth from the witness chair as he tenaciously cross-examined himself. At the conclusion of the trial he confessed his sins and complimented his attorney. "How could I possibly hide anythin' from such a mastermind?" he said impishly.

"One night during the Broadway run, Jimmy stormed into my dressing room all charged up," Merman recalled. "He was angrier than I'd ever seen him. I thought it was over something I had done. But it wasn't. Jimmy had just read that Father Coughlin had given a Nazi salute at some rally. 'Not only did he do that,' Jimmy yelled, 'but he told the people there that the only way to handle the Jews was to exterminate them.' " That night all through the performance, Jimmy was livid and kept muttering under his breath.

Father Charles E. Coughlin was a Canadian-born Roman Catholic priest whose weekly CBS broadcasts in the thirties attracted more than ten million regular listeners. A deep-voiced, impassioned speaker, he grew more political as the depression deepened. Each Sunday evening he lectured his audience about international Jewish bankers being responsible for all our economic ills, that President Roosevelt was part of a Communist conspiracy, that the Ku Klux Klan was justified in burning crosses. To those who didn't have access to a radio he published a magazine, *Social Justice*, which contained pro-Nazi and anti-Semitic articles.

Red, Hot and Blue! lasted 183 performances on Broadway, then moved to Chicago for a six week run. During its stay in the Windy City, Schnozzola did a late night stint at the Chez Paree nightclub. "Jeanne didn't come very often to watch her husband's act there," said Jackson. "One night she did. I wasn't around to see what happened but by the way Lou Clayton reported it, all hell broke loose. It seems that Jeanne was told that since she was Jimmy Durante's wife she could order anything she wanted free of charge. So she ordered imported caviar. Instead, she was served something else that was cheaper. She complained so loud that Jimmy ran out of his dressing room. He got to her table just as she emptied the plate over the waiter's head. Some of the slimy stuff landed on Jimmy's face. For a moment he was quiet but when it started trickling down to his nose he yelled, 'Nobody dare touch my probosciscator—only my wife.' Then he turned around and kissed her. But she was still sore and waltzed right out.''

In addition to appearing in the play and moonlighting at the Chez Paree, Jimmy participated in an experiment a science professor from the University of Chicago was conducting: "Does the size of the nose improve the smell?" Durante was instructed to sniff dozens of different foods while a machine hooked up to him registered the results. When the project was completed, he was given a certificate of appreciation. Proudly, he showed it off to Jackson who was always boasting that he had finished elementary school. "That's nothin'," said Jimmy. "This proves I'm nearly a college graduate!"

Chicago newspapers had written glowing stories about the experiment. Jimmy was more popular than ever. Crowds mobbed Durante so that he could hardly move. He was given a police escort to the railway station when he and Jeanne took the Twentieth Century Limited back to New York. There he was a headliner at Billy Rose's club, Casa Mañana.

Rose, who had a reputation for being parsimonious and a hardheaded business man, appeared to have different standards when dealing with Durante. He had once said, "Except for my wife, Fanny Brice, I regard Schnozzola as the country's finest comedian." He offered Jimmy free use of his Manhattan penthouse apartment, a chauffeur-driven Rolls Royce, and an open-ended contract to continue performing at the Casa Mañana. But before Jimmy had a chance to accept, Rose got embroiled in a major law suit and promptly forgot all about his generous proposal.

"Jimmy headed back to California determined that this time it would be different," said Jackson. "One thing about him is that he never gives up hope—no matter what happens, he always thinks there will change for the better. He was sure that now Hollywood would make good use of his talent, but he soon found out they still hadn't learned their lesson. They kept putting him in movies that were jinxed before they started. He did some beauties that even I had to admit were pretty hopeless."

To add to Durante's troubles, Lou Clayton was severely injured in an automobile accident as he was driving along Sunset Boulevard. Clayton's face was so badly cut that more than a dozen skin graft operations were necessary. When Jeanne heard that her husband was paying all the medical bills, she was furious. She relented slightly when she learned that Clayton, from his hospital bed, had arranged for Jimmy to work once again with Ethel Merman in a Broadway show called *Stars in Your Eyes*. However, she refused to accompany her husband to New York. When he arrived at the Astor Hotel, his usual Broadway address, the desk clerk handed him a telephone message. It was from Jeanne: "Tootis, all is forgiven. Break a leg."*

On February 9, 1939, the play opened at the Majestic Theater, where it played for four months. Although not as good as Jimmy's previous show it was well received by the critics. Typical was the review that appeared in the Brooklyn *Eagle*: "Broadway has a new musical that was made possible by Ethel Merman's lusty voice and Jimmy Durante's superb clowning. . . . The audience probably heard the anemic jokes before, but then you can't have everything."

Many of the jokes were indeed anemic:

Durante: Hello, is this the meat market?
Voice: Yeah.
Durante: Well, meet my wife at four o'clock.

*Break a leg is a show business expression for good luck.

121

Merman: Does this bus go over the Queensborough Bridge?
Durante: If it doesn't, we're goin' to get awful wet.

Durante: I ran into Professor Einstein today, an' how do you think I found him?
Merman: I don't know. How did you find him?
Durante: I pushed back his hair an' there he was.

Jeanne, who had remained in California during the run of the play, met her husband's train at the Los Angeles railroad station. She smelled of alcohol and was weaving so badly that she kept stumbling. A newspaper photographer who happened to be there clicked away. When he saw Schnozzola's sorrowful face, he removed the roll of film and silently handed it to him. Jeanne's solitary drinking had increased greatly. Durante found empty liquor bottles under the bed, in the kitchen cabinets, and crammed behind the living room radio.

Soon after he returned, Jeanne filed a complaint with the Los Angeles Superior Court. She charged that her husband often flew into violent rages and repeatedly resorted to striking her. A trial separation was agreed to—Jimmy was to pay $300 a week for support. The order was rescinded a few weeks later when the Durantes reconciled.

Like her husband, Jeanne seldom discussed their marriage. But she once confided to Maggie Arnold, their maid, "I exaggerated," she told her. "As you know, my Jimmy doesn't have it in him to hurt a fly. But sometimes I get so mad, I could scream."

"It wasn't so strange that Jeanne had confided to Maggie," Jackson said. "Maggie was more than a maid—she was part of the family. Jimmy looked to her to keep an eye on his wife. But the drinking didn't stop. It was almost as if Jeanne wanted to be caught."

A short time later Durante got another offer to do a Broadway play. This time he made Jeanne come along. "He was so pleased when she promised to go on the wagon," Jackson said, "he bought her an expensive pearl necklace."

The play, *Keep Off the Grass*, was a short lived musical review. Although the cast included some outstanding entertainers—Ray Bolger, Jane Froman, Ika Chase, and Jackie Gleason—it was a flop. Not even Jimmy's enthusiastic clowning could rescue it. Walter Winchell said, "It's simply not a good $4.40 buy."

Keep Off the Grass was inferior in music, dancing, and plot. Jimmy had a hodgepodge of roles. He was Dr. Kildare, a tree surgeon; President Franklin D. Roosevelt delivering a fireside chat in his B.V.D.s; the host of an intellectual radio quiz program that had monkeys on its panel; Romeo declaring his love to Juliet who was standing on a balcony scratching her poison ivy.

The play had equally imaginative writing. In one sequence, after canceling dates with five chorus girls, Schnozzola turned to the audience and said, "I have better things to do then messin' around with these dolls. Like strollin' down the boulevard in my Lucius Beebe clothes—a two-toned herringbone with a three button effect, a notched lapel with a red carnation stuck in it, a striped purple an' red ascot tie, an' settin' it off with tan reversed-calf shoes. . . . They don't call me Jimmy the well dressed man for nothin'!"

As soon as the show closed Jeanne made him take the next train to Los Angeles. It didn't matter to her that Jimmy had become a Hollywood pariah. "That's the only place I feel comfortable in," she told her husband. "I'm sure that you'll get something out there."

The only offer he got came from Republic Studios. In 1940, for a sum well below his customary contract, they reluctantly agreed to cast him in a Gene Autry horse opera, *Melody Ranch*. As tenderfoot Cornelius J. Courtney, recently from the East, he tried to saddle a horse. Having a great deal of trouble, he said, "I never rode a horse before." Then as he adjusted his brand new sombrero, he added, "An' neither has this horse. So we starts out even."

Melody Ranch didn't enhance his reputation. The word around town was that Durante was an aging comic trying to compete in a modern world. Clayton angrily pointed out that his client was only forty-eight-years-old and that his best days were still in front of him.

"That may be," said Mayer of MGM, "but I'm afraid I don't

see it that way. Personally, I like Schnozzola. However, in this business it's box office sales that count. And at this moment he just doesn't bring the cash customers in. All the other studios feel that same way."

They did. Each time Clayton tried to peddle Durante he got a turndown. It was only through the intervention of Jimmy's old friend, fellow comedian Phil Silvers, that he was hired by a major studio. Warner Brothers was anxious to star Silvers in *You're in the Army Now*. He insisted on getting Schnozzola to play his sidekick. Grudgingly, Warners took Durante on. The movie turned out to be superior to his previous pictures but unfortunately it was released on December 10, 1941, three days after Pearl Harbor. Reviewers didn't feel that movie viewers were ready to laugh about war.

Louis Cohen, who Schnozzola described as "My pal from the good days," had been a top movie executive and was now involved in major real estate transactions. He managed to get Jimmy several temporary nightclub jobs. "They didn't pay nearly as much as his former rate," Cohen said. "Another man would have complained bitterly. All Jimmy did was shrug his shoulders and look at me in his special way. 'I suppose them's the conditions that prevail,' " he'd say. 'It's a catostroke.' "

Durante was in the midst of performing in a theater-restaurant when he received a long-distance call from his sister's son in New York. "Grandpa had a heart attack," his nephew said. "The doctor doesn't expect him to live very much longer!" Bartolomeo's wife had died several years before and he was now living in Queens with his daughter, Lillian. That morning he had trimmed the hair of the parish priest and returned home appearing to be in good health. Suddenly, he collapsed. Bartolomeo was rarely sick. The last occasion was years before when he had suffered his only serious illness—ulcers. He claimed that a diet of garlic and lemon juice had promptly cured him. Now, it was apparent that no home remedy would be helpful. The doctor's diagnosis: severe hardening of the arteries as well as a hopeless heart condition.

Jimmy, who had always been close to his father, had visited him regularly. After the last meeting, he boasted to Jackson that the old man ate two bowls of minestrone, a heaping plate of spaghetti, and topped it off with a large slice of cheese cake.

"I just couldn't make myself believe that Pop was about to die," Schnozzola said. Contrary to the old adage about the show having to go on, Jimmy rushed to the airport still wearing makeup. He arrived at New York's Midtown Hospital just in time to clutch his father's hand. Minutes later the ninety-three-year-old man was pronounced dead.

Jimmy refused to leave the room. Finally, a nurse told him that he had to go so that the body could be taken to the morgue. Schnozzola who was unfamiliar with the word *morgue* thought it meant Bartolomeo would be buried in an unmarked grave in Potter's Field. "Please don't take Pop to no morgue!" he pleaded. "I'll pay. Please no morgue!" It took a great deal of convincing to make him understand that his father would have a proper burial.

Comeback Number One

The late thirties and early forties were Jimmy's most difficult years. "Someone with less moxie would have tossed in the towel," Jackson said. "Everything he touched seemed to be falling apart. From being one of the luckiest guys around, it starts to look like someone has put a curse on him. First there's a fire in his house. Then one on the movie set he's working and the film gets canceled. If that isn't bad enough, Jeanne gets real sick. It looks like the only people that still have faith in him are Lou and myself."

Schnozzola was badly in debt. So much so, that he had to borrow on his life insurance and pawn some of his wife's jewelry. Jeanne, who was now drinking openly, had lost a great deal of weight. She kept complaining of severe pains.

"Those years was the lowest point in my whole life," Durante said. "Not only was Jeannie in an' out of the hospital but her father and brother, Earl, passed away. So did my own father an' sister, Lily. I'm sittin' around at Lily's wake talkin' how good she an' Pop was when who do you think walks in? Jeannie! She looks like a ghost. Sick as she is she comes all the way from California. It's too much for her an' the next day she starts hemorrhagin'. I don't think I'll get her home alive—

she's that sick. But somehow me an' that gutsy gal makes it back to California. What's more she starts feelin' better—it's a miracle! She's almost like her old self—sweet and obligin'. We even start goin' out again."

During the 1942 Christmas week the Durantes had dinner at Beverly Hills' Trocadero with Harry James, a prominent jazz musician, and his bride-to-be, actress Betty Grable. This was during World War II and Betty had just been voted by GIs as the pinup girl they'd most like to be marooned with. Schnozzola was selected the neighbor they'd most like to live next door to.

"Betty and I often spoke about that meal," said James. "And not because of the food—it was what Schnozzola did. 'Maybe those soldiers won't want me for a neighbor when they hear I walk in my sleep,' he told us. Then he closed his eyes, made snoring sounds, put his hands in front of him, and walked out the door onto Sunset Boulevard. I was too fascinated to move, but Jeanne and Betty told me to go after him. I did. There he was on Sunset with his hands still stretched in front of him. He was finally stopped by a policeman. Mind you, Jimmy continued pretending to be asleep. The cop started shaking him, but when he realized who it was, he began to apologize. 'Gee, Schnozzola, I'm sorry. In the dark I didn't know it was you. Can I call a patrol car to take you home?' I was able to convince him that it was all a gag and that Jimmy was with me. As we left to go back to the Troc, the cop said, 'Schnozzola, me and the missus think you're the funniest man alive. Wait until I tell her about this!'"

Now that Jeanne seemed to be on the mend, Jimmy accepted two guest spots on the "Camel Caravan" radio show, which was broadcast live from New York. He also agreed to appear at the Copacabana. The two concurrent jobs would bring him $11,000. "You can't imagine how happy I was," Durante said. "Things seemed to be changin' for the better. But on the taxi ride to the radio station I get this feelin' that somethin' bad is about to happen. Natural, I think it means I'll bomb on the air. But it ain't that because I did pretty good. So after the show I call Jeannie in California. I remember her exact words. She tells me, 'Tootis, I liked the program very much. You'll be pleased to know my mother's with me an' I'm feelin' fine.'"

Durante was so delighted that he decided to sleep late— something he hadn't done in a long while. He told the Hotel Astor desk clerk not to disturb him until noon. However, very early the next morning he was awakened by a long-distance phone call from his mother-in-law. "Jeannie is dead," was all she said. A severe heart ailment had ended the Durante's twenty-two-year marriage.

"Jimmy was still afraid of flying," said Jackson. "But he took the first flight he could get. Remember it was wartime and he got bumped off in Salt Lake City to make room for a soldier. It happened once more before he finally reached Los Angeles. I'm pretty sure if he had told them the reason for his traveling, he'd have been allowed to keep his seat. But he was much too miserable to say anything."

As soon as the plane landed, Durante went to the mortuary where the body had been taken. He knelt beside the coffin and said the rosary over and over. For two days and nights he refused to leave. "I tried to make him go out for a meal or a fresh shirt," the funeral director said. "Mr. Durante wouldn't budge. When a loved one passes on, it's not unusual for the living to behave irrationally. But Mr. Durante was an extreme case. I don't think that man moved a muscle in all the time he was there. Didn't eat! Didn't talk! Just sat and stared."

On February 17, 1943, three days after her death, Jeanne was buried in Arcadia, California's Mountain View Cemetery, next to her father and brother. Jimmy was so dazed while the priest was speaking that he almost fell into the open grave. After the interment, Clayton cautioned him that if he wished to retain his sanity he had to go back to work. "You must!" his friend pleaded. "That's the only way you'll keep from going to pieces. You have to start working again. The Copacabana wants to headline you. You always enjoyed working there and it's probably the leading nightclub in the country. Everybody who counts goes there."

"Let me think about it," Durante replied. "Right now I

want mostly to be alone." Reluctantly, he allowed one of his cousins, Frank Ross, to spend the nights with him.

"I didn't get much sleep," Ross said. "Neither did he. All night long he'd wander from room to room looking at snapshots, Jeanne's dresses, her shoes. Anything that belonged to her. He'd keep saying, 'If only I'd stayed home with her it might never have happened.' I tried to reason with him but he'd turn away while I'd be speaking. He'd act like some kind of zombie so it was impossible to tell if I was getting through to him. Evidently I had because one night he said, 'If the Copa still wants me I'll go to New York.' "

The Copacabana, on 10 East Sixtieth Street, was regarded as the Mecca of nightclubs. Over the years it had become a universal landmark. Frank Sinatra, who frequently appeared there had said, "You're a show business nobody until you make the Copa and do three shows nightly under its tremendous pastel roof."

"Durante's Copacabana engagement made nightclub history," said Abel Green, who had become the editor of *Variety* after Silverman's retirement. "There's been nothing like it. The place was so crowded with adoring fans they literally hung from the rafters. They applauded, whistled, cheered, and roared. Schnozzola wasn't allowed to leave the floor; good-naturedly he granted encore after encore."

He packed them in so deep that the customers were more than satisfied to get a table behind a post. Looking perplexed, as only he could, Jimmy told the audience, "Last night I accidentally dropped a collar button from my shirt on the floor. An' before I can pick it up a waiter throws a tablecloth right over it an' seats six people."

Copacabana employees were delighted each time Durante performed there. "We could count on getting bigger tips," said headwaiter Joe Lopez. "Schnozzola put the customers in such a good mood that they all wanted to share their pleasure with us. One night an intoxicated patron who had been applauding Jimmy wildly beckoned me to his table. 'What's the biggest tip you ever received?' he asked me. 'Two hundred dollars,' I replied. 'Well, here's $300,' said the tipsy man as he handed me three crisp hundred dollar bills. Then he drained his glass as he said, 'The next time someone asks you that question, tell them it was $300 and that I was the one who gave it to you. By the way, who gave you that $200 tip?' He almost smashed the glass when I said, 'You did, sir. It was the last time Schnozzola performed here.' "

Night after night the drums rolled, the horns blared the opening notes of "Inka Dinka Doo" and out came a very enthusiastic Durante. He made no pretense of offering the customers anything new. Some nights he was joined by his two old partners, Eddie Jackson and Lou Clayton. The Three Sawdust Bums were back on Broadway. The jokes were the same, and the same old Schnozzola made them come alive.

Durante: My cousin the magician has terrible luck.

Jackson: That's too bad.

Durante: For twenty years he's been sawing a woman in half.

Jackson: Did his saw finally slip?

Durante: No. It's because he always ends up with the half that eats.

Durante: My wife stayed up after one last night.

Jackson: Why?

Durante: I was the one she was after!

Durante: I'm pretty smart if I say so myself.

Jackson: Why do you think that?

Durante: Well, this afternoon I went into a fruit store an' the clerk thought I was some kind of out-of-town hick. But I fooled him.

Jackson: How?

Durante: "Those two apples will cost you two dollars each," he tells me. That's when I outsmart him. I hand over a five dollar bill. As he's about to give me a dollar change, I say "Keep it, we're even. On the way in I stepped on a grape."

Initially, Jimmy had been hired for two weeks, but he was such a hit that the Copacabana management gave him a substantial raise and held him over for three additional months. The little man with the big nose had reaffirmed his place as one of the great clowns of the era. Lucrative feelers poured in from Hollywood, radio, and nightclubs. MGM offered him a five-year contract to appear in two pictures a year at $75,000 each. Clayton made them up the ante to $150,000 for one picture a year. He also secured permission from them to allow Jimmy to perform elsewhere.

A short while later Schnozzola signed another five-year contract. This one was with the Camel cigarette company. For $5,000 a week he agreed to co-star with comedian Garry Moore in a weekly radio program. Moore, whose humor was much more sophisticated, was the perfect counterpart for Durante. Jimmy described his new partner as, "A smart kid with a crew haircut an' lots of classy brains."

Since there was a twenty-two-year difference in their ages and because of Durante's constant reference to "Junior— that's my boy," many listeners thought they were father and son. The format seldom varied. Moore was the master of ceremonies. After delivering a short monologue—often about a tragic love affair—Durante would come out yelling and sing one of his involved songs. Then he and Moore would do a long comedy sketch. One of the funniest was when Moore zipped through a description of his former occupation at top speed.

"Jimmy," he said, "I used to work in Wauwatosa, Wisconsin, in the water works, as a reasonably reliable referee for the refrigerator wreckers, recluses, and renegades."

A few minutes later, a guest asked Durante what Moore's job had been before he became an actor. Schnozzola made several attempts to repeat it. After badly mangling his last effort he said wearily, "Junior was some kind of Jim-of-all-trades!"

It was on the show that Durante introduced a mythical friend, Umbriago. No one except Schnozzola ever saw this secret pal who had either just left or was about to arrive. Umbriago came partly from Jimmy's imagination and partly from Italian folklore—a happy little man who was the life of the party. During World War II, paratroopers shouted "Umbriago" before jumping. Combat journalists reported that marines yelled, "Umbriago, dat's my boy!" when storming an invasion beach.

Jimmy once received a letter from a mournful mother whose son had been killed in Iwo Jima. "Dear Schnozzola," the woman wrote. "My only son just gave his life for his country. I suppose I should be proud of that fact, but I'm afraid it's much too soon for me to take any comfort in it. Michael was my pride and joy. The reason I'm writing to you is to extend my thanks for your giving him so much pleasure in his very brief life. He'd watch your program religiously and laugh and laugh.... His friend, a fellow marine, just telephoned to tell me about Michael's death. It seems that just before his life ended he yelled, 'Umbriago.' Then died with the smile still on his face.... Thanks."

As a rule Durante wrote very few letters. His explanation was that because of a full schedule he lacked the time. Eddie Jackson didn't agree: "The truth was that Jimmy was afraid to write them because he was embarrassed he'd make too many mistakes. But in this case he immediately sent one to the woman. About his being glad he made her son so happy. That the dead boy had been a brave marine and had a brave mother."

Screen actress Greer Garson was scheduled to appear as a guest on the show. While waiting for the program to start she asked to be introduced to Umbriago. When told by Jimmy that he was out of town visiting his sick grandmother, Garson, who was well known in Hollywood for her sophistication and courtliness, said, "Such fidelity is admirable. It must be catching."

"Yeah," Durante replied. "An' he's also got chicken pox." Before she arrived, he had warned the staff to mind their manners. "Miss Garson is a high class lady who comes from England," he said. "So be polite while she's around!"

Garson had rehearsed her lines carefully, but still had doubts. "Jimmy," she said, "I'm not used to comedy. What happens if I fail to say my lines correctly?"

"In that case, Miss Garson," he replied, "we'll both go down the toilet." Quickly, he remembered his etiquette lecture. "Pardon me, Miss Garson," he said blushing. "I didn't mean it like it came out."

The actress smiled as she touched his cheek. "You were quite right," she said. "I'd best rehearse again."

During this period, Schnozzola collapsed from exhaustion and was briefly hospitalized. The doctors told him that it had been caused by his heavy work schedule plus the fact that he still hadn't gotten over Jeanne's death. They advised lots of sleep, a revised diet, and a much-needed vacation. He managed it to get away to Clear Lake for exactly one night.

"Too many memories," was all he said when asked why the holiday had been so brief. Grudgingly, he took vitamin pills. "Vitaphones" he called them. But when it came to performing he still didn't spare himself.

"I don't think he knew how to sit down and relax," said Jackson. "Whenever he was told to take it easy, he'd say, 'We'll be resting in our graves for a long time. So while we're still alive we should keep hoppin' around.' That man is a human dynamo!"

Eddie Davis, a leading comedy writer, shared Jackson's assessment of Durante. "He's on the go all the time," Davis said. "Maybe that's the secret of his amazing draw. I've written for the best in show business: Eddie Cantor, Will Rogers, Jack Benny, Bob Hope, Bing Crosby. I don't want to put any of them down, but Schnozzola belongs in a class by himself. I'd give him an A plus for his special kind of zing."

Durante felt that Eddie Davis also deserved an outstanding rating. Whenever Jimmy wanted fresh material, he turned to Davis, a New York taxi driver turned "hack writer"—his own joke. The fact that Davis couldn't spell or write proper English endeared him to Schnozzola. He'd frequently talk about Davis's start in show business. The future comedy writer would follow Eddie Cantor around Manhattan in his taxicab. When they both stopped for a red light, Davis would shout out original jokes. They were so good that Cantor gave him fifty dollars a week to sit home and compose amusing one-liners. Within a year Cantor was paying him $1,250 a week. With Cantor's blessing, the former cab driver started branching out. He was the author of *Road to Morocco* and numerous stage hit musicals. Among them: *Follow the Girls* and *Ankles Aweigh.*

"I worked for a lot of different guys," said Davis. "But it's God's truth that I'd get the most pleasure from writing for Jimmy even if he kept changing my words upside down. I once asked Garry Moore to name the three funniest men in show business. Without blinking an eye he answered, 'Durante! Durante! Durante!' "

Moore like Davis was adulatory in his praise. "Everything Schnozzola did was funny," he said. "In front of the mike or away from it. One night the eminent composer and critic, Deems Taylor, came backstage after a broadcast. Deems was a great fan of Jimmy's and wanted to meet him. Schnozzola, as it turned out, had never heard of him. I escorted Taylor into Jimmy's dressing room. 'Jimmy,' I said. 'I'd like you to meet Deems Taylor.' Schnozzola stuck out his hand and said, 'Whose?' "

Now that Durante was once again a big name as well as an eligible bachelor, he was considered an extremely good catch. Dozens of extremely pretty show girls made it obvious they were available. In 1944, during one of his appearances at the Copacabana, he met twenty-three-year-old Margie Little, a combination switchboard-hat check girl. "I was right away smittened by her good looks," Jimmy admitted. "Also by her brains. Not only was she pretty but smart, too. Why, when she was very young she'd already been picked Miss New Jersey State Fair. The judges begged her to try out for Miss America because they were sure she'd go all the way. But she decides to go to business school an' ends up at the Copa answerin' the switchboard."

In addition to a lovely, finely chiseled face, flaming red hair, and an excellent figure, Margie Little possessed an extremely high IQ. Jimmy boasted that Copacabana employees would bring their problems to her for solutions. "The way she doped them out was like a regular Solomon from the Bible," he said. "I liked being around her and sometimes we'd go out steady."

134

Jackson felt that although Margie was frequently mistaken for Jimmy's daughter, they were a perfectly matched couple. "She told me once," said Jackson, "that she loved Jimmy because he was kind and decent. Those two agreed on most everything except getting married. I'd never seen him so happy until he'd start thinking about Jeanne. Then he'd feel guilty—that it was disloyal to her memory if he got married again. Pretty soon the whole avenue was talking about it."

"Why doesn't Schnozzola get hitched to the lady?" asked Walter Winchell. "She's an A-one-plus catch. But I'll lay fifty to one that he never pops the question. Jimmy Durante has become a confirmed bachelor."

"Winchell was right in calling Jimmy that," said Jackson. "He seemed afraid of another failed marriage. The first one had been so bad that he was scared of trying matrimony again. He seemed happiest when he had his men pals around him. His house was like an all-male club with him as the president. Not that he wanted to be surrounded by yes men or that he insisted on being boss. But we all knew he was the main breadwinner and so we allowed him to call the shots."

In 1947, Garry Moore decided to strike out on his own. Rexall Drugs, the show's new sponsor, signed Jimmy to carry on alone. He remained for three more years. With Don Ameche as his straight man, and with Davis's contributions, he continued to exhilarate listeners on the weekly "Jimmy Durante Show." A story in the *Saturday Evening Post* revealed that Schnozzola had not only retained his popularity but had increased it. "He could read the telephone book and make it entertaining," the article said.

Jimmy would still sing a few bars of "Inka Dinka Doo," halt and shout, "Stop the Music! There's something wrong with the orchestral harmonics!" Most of the radio audience had never seen Jimmy in person, but that didn't matter—he was able to transmit his "this is the way it is" frustration over the air waves.

John Crosby, the radio critic for the New York *Herald Tribune* said, "Schnozzola blows his lines with such wild glee that he's quickly becoming our leading radio comedian. I'll be listening to him in my living room and want to reach out to pet him. He's that endearing."

General Dwight Eisenhower was another Durante devotee. While president of Columbia University he sent Jimmy a fan note that expressed his feelings: "Mamie and I haven't had the pleasure of meeting you firsthand, our radio had to suffice. . . . I want you to know that we refuse all invitations on the night you're on the wire."

Eisenhower may have also been partially responsible for Jimmy's return to making movies. Attending a dinner party, the general was seated next to the wife of a leading film executive. "You have to be blind not to notice Schnozzola's talents," he told her.

This time around, Hollywood was much kinder—at least at the beginning. Jimmy was given suitable roles that displayed his unique offbeat talent. "Schnozzola is rejuvenated," said Hedda Hopper. "At long last he's buckled down and become an accomplished screen comedian."

Hopper may have missed the real reason: The film studios finally realized that the public wanted to watch an uninhibited Durante use his own special brand of comedy. The public did not want to see him strangled by a bad script that was doomed from the outset. Now, in rapid order he gave a series of sparkling screen performances. Critics lauded Durante and called his comedy sequences, "Colossal . . . Exalted . . . Superior."

Jimmy was very pleased when Margie Little moved to Hollywood. She decided to try movies when producer Joseph Pasternak signed her to appear in Durante's movie, *Two Sisters from Boston*. "I was thrilled to be working alongside Jimmy," she said. "I wrote to my family to be sure and see the movie and to listen carefully to my one line. They saw it four times but couldn't find me. Jimmy had been afraid to tell me that it had been cut out." Margie's movie career ended but the romance didn't. They continued to be what Winchell called "an item."

In October of 1946, Jimmy was immortalized in concrete

when Sid Grauman, owner of Hollywood's famous Chinese Theater, pushed the celebrated nose into wet cement. "The usual procedure," Grauman said, "was to get the star's footprints and handprints. But in Jimmy's case the obvious choice was his schnozzle. It's since become one of our biggest attractions."

"Things were moving along swell," said Jackson. "Everything was clicking. Then all of a sudden he got the bad news: a growth on his lower intestine!"

21

The Big C Scare

Late in December of 1947, Durante was preparing to go on a seventeen-city fund-raising tour for the March of Dimes. Just before he was ready to leave, Clayton insisted he get a physical examination. "Eddie tells me that you recently started complaining of cramps," he said. "I want you to get a checkup."

"I just had one an' the doc gave me a clean bill-of-fare," Jimmy replied.

"That's fine," Clayton answered. "Still I want you to go!"

Schnozzola knew better than to argue with Clayton. "No one in a right mind ever did," said Durante. "He was like a Coney Island lifesaver savin' a drownin' person. They better do everythin' he says or he'll push them back in the water."

X rays revealed a small growth on Jimmy's lower intestine; surgery was imperative. On December thirty-first he checked into the hospital. "It was the first time in years that Jimmy wasn't headlining on New Year's Eve," Jackson said. "But even his being in the hospital didn't stop him. That evening, with the operation staring him smack in the face, he went from ward to ward so he could entertain the patients."

When Durante returned to his room, he was greeted by

Margie Little, Lou Clayton, and Eddie Jackson. Soon as he entered, he took a sealed envelope from the nightstand and handed it to Jackson.

"With unusual quietness," Jackson recalled, "he told us it was instructions in case he didn't come back. The way he said it made me decide to remain at the hospital all night. I sat near his bed and about four in the morning he sat bolt-up and I could see tears in his eyes. 'It's probably the Big Casino,' he said, 'so I got to wondering what would have happened to me all these years without you fellows. I'd like to live long enough to pay back what I owe.'"

A few hours later the tumor was removed—it was benign. When Durante was wheeled back into his room he found Jackson and Clayton waiting for him. "I didn't run out on you this time," he said weakly. "I'm a very, very lucky guy."

The following day Jackson returned the sealed envelope Jimmy had given him on New Year's Eve. "I hope it's a hundred years before you hand me something like this," he said.

"You didn't read it?" asked Durante.

"No, Jimmy," Jackson replied. "But I got the idea that it took care of all of us."

"Naw," said an embarrassed Schnozzola. "It was only a tip on a horse."

Shortly after the cancer scare Jimmy talked to a writer for *Guideposts*, a religious publication. "If I didn't have that operation," he said, "that polyp could have gone malignant and I'm in real trouble. But God is really with me. When I wake up from the antiseptic, I see this St. Christopher medal around my neck. I ask the nurse where it came from? She answers, 'While you're sleeping, a nice lady with gray hair comes in, says a prayer and puts it on you.'"

From then on Jimmy always wore it on a chain along with three other religious ornaments: a medal of the Madonna that had been given to him by his father, a medal of the Crucifixion that Jeanne had purchased when they were married, and a miniature cross that had belonged to his mother. "When Mama was alive, God rest her soul," Jimmy said, "I'd always follow her to church to find out where God is. I still follow her."

All his life Durante was deeply religious. When he learned that I was a Quaker, he wanted to know all about silent worship. I took him to a Friends Meeting. That Sunday all of the spoken messages concerned children. He seemed to frown as he listened to them. Later, I asked him what he had been thinking. "Kids," he replied, "they have to be taught to hate, an' that ain't a religious way. When I was in God's hands in the hospital, that feelin' came to me."

Now that Schnozzola knew that his career wasn't going to end prematurely, his chief concern was the radio program. How could he do it? The doctors had told him that he must eliminate all work for several months. He needn't have worried as some of the nation's top comedians volunteered to stand in for him. Among them: Bob Hope, Al Jolson, Frank Morgan, Red Skelton. When they told listeners that Jimmy was convalescing, he received hundreds of get-well cards. One that he especially liked came from Laurence Olivier. The British actor had scrawled, "Do recover to bring us more joy. Schnozzola dat's my boy."

When Clayton felt that Durante was strong enough to resume work, he granted permission. "I think I could have gone back lots earlier," Jimmy said, "but Lou nixed the idea. He took better care of me then himself."

Soon after Jimmy's reappearance on the radio show, one of the skits was devoted to vigorousness. "There's still plenty of energy left in this boy," Schnozzola said. "Why, just yesterday I swung a baseball bat so hard it broke into a thousand pieces.

"That must have been a sight to behold," said Don Ameche, his current partner. "Then what happened?"

"I bought some hot dogs with sauerkraut an' some of it stuck in my teeth," Jimmy replied.

"That's too bad but what has that to do with baseball?" Ameche asked.

"I used those smashed baseball bat pieces for toothpicks," said Jimmy.

"The way he looked when he answered me," said Ameche, "was pure Schnozzola. Even the usually sullen makeup lady laughed. We had a live audience watching that show. They were so elated by that bit of nonsense they kept stamping their feet and pounding each other on the back."

It was quite different when Durante returned to Hollywood. "I thought things had changed," said Jackson. "But it was the same old merry-go-round."

The studios resumed their old policy of putting Durante into low-priority movies and not allowing him to improvise. His next three pictures were such box-office flops that his film contract wasn't renewed.

Billy Rose, a long time Durante fan, was so incensed that he wrote an open letter to Jimmy's former bosses: "When you gave him a suitable role, rather than a jack-in-the-box specialty act, he set fire to the celluloid, but soon your hired hands were using him to prop up every crippled script on the lot. . . . Please tell your hired day laborers out there that when they mess up with Jimmy, they're messing with the best loved guy in show business. If they cool him off again, strong men will come down from the mountains and up from the valleys and turn your studio into a bowling alley."

Jimmy didn't pay attention to any adverse criticism; he was much too concerned with Lou Clayton's health. Early in 1950, Clayton began complaining of chest pains, but refused to visit a doctor. "I'm afraid of what they'll tell me," he said. The tables were now turned—it was Durante who forced his old partner to seek medical advice. Before it was given, Clayton stormed out of the doctor's office. Instead, Jimmy was told the grim news: his "bestest best friend" was dying from cancer.

A malignant stomach ulcer had been discovered. The cancerous cells had spread so wildly that it was felt surgery might prolong Clayton's life slightly, but chances for survival were almost nonexistent. Jimmy persuaded him to be operated on, and for the next five months he watched Clayton waste away—his weight went down from 166 pounds to less than a hundred. Once again Durante paid all the medical bills. He also acceded to most of the doomed man's whims. One afternoon Clayton asked Jimmy to take him to Las Vegas. "I feel that we'll break the bank," he said.

"We didn't break no bank," Schnozzola said. "But it was good to see what pleasure he got out of rollin' the dice. Everytime he'd win a few dollars, he'd let out a yell. It wasn't really so loud like a yell, more like a pussycat sound. Still it was loud music to my ears."

Despite his condition, Clayton continued to supervise Durante's career. "Television is the coming thing," he kept telling him. "You'll be a natural in it. They need you badly." Whenever Jimmy expressed doubts, Clayton was livid. "Your trouble is that you don't realize how good you are!" he'd say.

During Clayton's last days, he became very sentimental. "I have a strong hunch that my number is about to come up," he told one visitor. "I want to raise a monument to my pal Jimmy Durante. There's nobody as sweet as he is, or as great. In a bad world he's stayed good. This crazy age that produced us sent lots of fellows to Sing Sing, but something inside that man kept him good and honest and kind. When you're near him it's like warming your hands over a fire."

Clayton died on the morning of September 12, 1950. Actor George Jessel delivered the eulogy. He finished by quoting some of Clayton's last words: "Take care of the long-nosed fellow. If I ever hear of anyone hurting Jimmy, I'll come back and kill him!"

Comeback Number Two

Jimmy was lost without Clayton's guidance. "Lou was my eyes an' ears," he said. "More than that he was even my feet. I never took a step without askin' him first." During the years Clayton served as Durante's manager he had a strict rule: *Always ask for at least double the offer!* He felt that since his client was the funniest man in show business, prospective employers should be made to pay handsomely. The fact that Durante had fizzled in Hollywood didn't discourage him. His reasoning was simple: *If the film studios weren't smart enough to use Jimmy properly someone wiser should be given the opportunity.*

Clayton had started giving serious thought to television when Ted Mack of the "Major Bowes Amateur Hour" told him that Schnozzola-imitators were repeatedly awarded top honors. "The wheel of fortune goes around and around," he said to Jackson. "It should be made to stop right here! We've got the real thing, not some fake copy!"

Durante, who had never fully accepted moving pictures or radio, was reluctant to switch to the new medium. He believed that a true comic needed the intimacy of a nightclub. "Drunken hecklers, soup-spillin' waiters, an' curvy cigarette gals snappin' your picture," he felt were essential for a superior performance.

"He started to have different thoughts about TV when Clayton died," said Jackson. "For weeks after Lou's death Jimmy remained at home refusing to speak to anyone—it was even worse than it had been when Jeanne passed away. If he did say something it was only, 'Let me be. I'm thinking!' After a month of living like a hermit he called me up. 'I've decided that television is what Lou would have wanted for me. Call around.' "

Abe Lastfogel, a leading entertainment agent, arranged for Durante to appear on NBC-TV. Lastfogel, president of the William Morris theatrical agency, was a legend in show business. He was famous for arranging giant deals. Vice President Hubert H. Humphrey had once said, "If ever I forsake politics for the stage, the first thing I'll do is get Abe Lastfogel for my agent!"

Lastfogel's client list read like a *Who's Who* of show business. It included Danny Thomas, Dinah Shore, Mickey Rooney, Betty Hutton, and Ray Bolger. Bob Burns, who was known as the "Bazooka Man," once told Jimmy, "I have total faith in Lastfogel. If Abe tells me to jump out of the top floor of a skyscraper window, I'd do it because I know he'll have a net on the floor below all set to catch me."

"With a recommendation like that I took Lastfogel's word," Jimmy said. Durante made his television debut in October 1950 on NBC's "Four Star Review." He alternated being the host with comedians Ed Wynn, Danny Thomas, and Jack Carson.* He was an immediate success. His initial performance was acclaimed by critics as a classic example of how a television show should be put together. The New York *Post* called him "TV's newest and freshest face." At the time he was fifty-seven years old.

Jimmy's television bosses wisely allowed him to wander from the prepared script. In a hotel sequence he stared disap-

---

* The name of the show was later changed to the "All Star Review." Subsequent TV programs were the "Colgate Comedy Hour" and "The Jimmy Durante Show."

provingly at his sparsely furnished room and ad-libbed, "There's a pickpocket in this hotel!" He then reached for the telephone and yelled, "Room service send up an order of furniture for a person who's young in heart." A moment later a waiter appeared wheeling a baby crib. Jimmy looked at him fiercely. "If you try to burp me," he said in his famous hoarse delivery, "I'll murder you!" The surprised waiter fled for the men's room.

John Wayne had a similar experience when he was invited to appear on Jimmy's program. "Schnozzola thought he was being helpful by tossing me cues for the skit we were doing," Wayne said. "The only trouble was that he was feeding me cues from the second skit while we were still in the middle of the first one. I finally managed to get through to him. Remember, this was in the days when most TV shows were still live. Now that he realized what he had done I was sure that things would be smoother. Was I wrong! He started tossing out original lines he had just made up—they were even harder to follow. I didn't attempt to—I just leaned back and roared. Later when I mentioned it he looked surprised. 'Do you think it makes a difference what we say?' he asked. 'Most words are pretty much the same.' To Jimmy I doubt if it made a difference. His charm was his complete innocence."

The show became fresher and funnier when Schnozzola grew restive and started tearing the script apart. After a particularly incongruous improvisation, he'd shrug his shoulders and remark, "That brings the television set a little bit closer." When he and the English language collided—as they invariably did—Durante would graciously admit defeat. "That time I just didn't split the infinitive," he'd say cheerfully. "I broke it into little pieces!"

His faulty syntax was never more apparent than when Helen Traubel, a leading prima donna at the Metropolitan Opera, was his guest. The assistant director of his program thought Traubel would be an interesting visitor because she and Schnozzola were so different. When her appearance was proposed, Jimmy said, "I suppose she sings on key, but what bothers me is if she's able to strut?"

"My curiosity was piqued when I was told about his reaction," Traubel said. "I watched the program to learn what strut was and I practiced in the privacy of my bedroom. When I felt that I was ready for Jimmy Durante, I agreed to be on the show. I had no idea what I was in for."

John Crosby, the New York *Herald Tribune* critic, called it "Television's finest hour." When the statuesque Wagnerian singer strode on stage in full armor, Durante gasped and ad-libbed, "Holy smoke, she's been drafted!"

"From that moment on the show really sparkled," said Crosby. "Their duet of "Our Voices Were Meant For Each Other" and the silly but wonderful wisecracks were pure gems."

Traubel told Jimmy that she loved to read nonfiction. "Then we have lots in common besides our singin'," he said. "I also love nonfriction." Later in the show when Traubel donned a skirt and blouse he attempted to pin a corsage on her ample bosom. He was very embarrassed and wound up tacking it to the back of her skirt. "Don't sit down!" he shouted. But his warning had come a moment too late as she settled in a chair.

"Ouch!" she yelped. "I've just been stuck on my backside!"

"What we have to do for a livin'," Schnozzola said. "It's humiliatin'!"

"There are some compensations in life," Traubel said. When she realized that Durante hadn't understood her, she attempted to explain. "Listening to classical music is one of the pleasures allowed us," she said.

"Oh, I know all about that kind of music," he replied. "The *Moonlight Sinatra* is one of them."

The program was such a success that Jimmy decided to get other "classy" visitors. "Greta Garbo would be swell," he told his producer. "I know her from the old days when our movie sets were right next to each other." He sent the reclusive movie queen a personal letter. A few days later he received a reply.

"Dear Mr. Schnozzola," Garbo wrote. "Of course I remember you. Fondly. You are that dear man who made me laugh so. But I'm afraid that I cannot accept your kind invitation.

I'm not yet ready for television, but thank you for asking me. Your friend Greta Garbo."

Most of the guests were far removed from Jimmy's world of "deese" and "dem." That didn't stop him from singing "high-falutin" duets with Margaret Truman, Lily Pons, and Patrice Munsel; accompanying the very aristocratic Ethel Barrymore on the piano as they both played ragtime; swapping slapstick routines with drama actress Bette Davis. After that program, Davis told him, "Jimmy, you were a barrel of fun."

"Likewise," answered Durante. "You're a barrel yourself."

"Good gracious," said a shocked Davis. "I know that I've been putting on weight, but I had no idea it was that obvious!"

Always the gentleman, Jimmy tried to assure her that he hadn't intended it that way. "What I mean," he said comfortingly, "is that you're like a laughin' hyena."

Often, his writers tried to slip in off-color jokes. When Schnozzola spotted them in time, they were removed. However, he didn't always recognize them until it was too late. On one program he evaluated screen actress Lana Turner's shape. Turner was frequently referred to as the "Sweater Girl" because of the alluring way she filled one out.

"Take away her sweater," Jimmy said, "and what have you got?" Ed Sullivan ballyhooed the double entendre comment in his column. An embarrassed Durante telephoned Lana Turner in Madrid where she was making a movie. "I apologize," he told her. "I should have my mouth washed out with soap!"

At the end of the first year Schnozzola was presented with the George Foster Peabody Award for television excellence; a *Motion Picture Daily* poll named him TV's Best Performer; TV critics voted him the year's outstanding personality; delighted NBC executives gave him a large, handmade silver door knocker that was inscribed: "Our Oscar to you, Jimmy."

Durante always ended his program with a subdued, emotional sigh. He'd immediately follow it with an intimate stage whisper, "Good night, Mrs. Calabash, wherever you are." The response, which had been generous when he used this sign off on radio, increased tremendously when he switched to television. Formerly, he had received several dozen letters begging him to reveal Mrs. Calabash's identity. The number swelled to several hundred when he repeated his Calabash farewell on TV. His voice took on a tender, emotional depth as he bid the mysterious woman good night. Now, in addition to hearing him, the audience could watch a wistful Schnozzola deliver the memorable line.

John Crosby, the New York *Herald Tribune* critic, called it, "The most sensitive and unparalleled farewell on the tube . . . Mrs. Calabash whoever you may be, you're a very lucky lady to be remembered so lovingly."

When reporters asked Jimmy who she was, he'd wink mischievously and say, "That's my secret. I want it to rest where it is." The more he refused to tell, the greater the interest.

Gossip columnist Louella Parsons announced that she had learned the inside story: "Jimmy and his late wife, Jeanne, were driving to California from New York when they passed a quaint, little village named Calabash. Mrs. Durante fell so in love with the place she talked about it incessantly. Durante started calling his wife 'Mrs. Calabash.' "

Jimmy was asked if her account was accurate. He refused to confirm or deny it. "It's not nice to doubt a lady," he said. "If that's what Louella claims it's strictly her own business!" He softened his statement a few weeks later when Margaret Truman appeared on his show. "Miss Truman tells me her father is one of my steady fans an' wants to know who Mrs. Calabash is. So if a President wants to know I guess you can't blame Louella so much for trying.' "

Other prominent guesses were:

- Mrs. Calabash was the name of a racehorse that always finished last causing Schnozzola to lose thousands of dollars. This was his way of showing that he wasn't carrying a grudge.
- Mrs. Calabash was Jimmy's nickname for his old partner, Lou Clayton.
- Mrs. Calabash was the widowed mother of a small boy

who had died from polio. During the youngster's last days he would always watch Uncle Jimmy's show.

- Mrs. Calabash was a former neighbor who twenty years before had told her family she was going out to buy a pack of cigarettes. She never returned.
- Mrs. Calabash was the married name of an old girlfriend who had jilted Durante in favor of a dentist from the Bronx.

The truth is that Mrs. Calabash was the brainchild of Phil Cohan, producer of Jimmy's radio show. Cohan said that he and Durante created Mrs. Calabash as a fictional joke. They got the name from the type of pipe Cohan was smoking. After building up the audience's curiosity they planned to reveal the truth on a subsequent program. Shortly before it was going to happen, Jimmy was visiting several monks at a Catholic monastery. The Mrs. Calabash routine came up in the conversation. Durante confessed that it was a gag and that he planned to explain it on his next show. The monks were horrified. They pointed out that most people had come to believe Mrs. Calabash was a real person. Exposing her as a comic hoax would destroy the warm and touching image he had established.

"We decided to keep Mrs. Calabash," Cohan said. "We realized that we had a good thing going for us. I'm glad we did because the fan letters kept pouring in. The Dallas chapter of the Junior League asked us if Mrs. Calabash could become their mascot, a Girl Scout troop in Boston wanted her to become their Brownie leader and a young music student who lived in England wanted her to become his patron."

A new generation had discovered Durante. I had personal evidence of that appeal when I accompanied Jimmy on a shopping expedition in search of a sweater. "I want one just like Rex Harrison wore in *My Fair Lady*," he said. "Rex told me the best place to find one in New York is the Water and Sons store on Franklin Avenue. Naturally, Schnozzola had the name and address slightly twisted: it was Brooks Brothers on Madison Avenue.

We had met in the Brill Building on Broadway. Since it was a lovely autumn day I suggested that we walk. It turned out to be a mistake. We hadn't gone more than ten feet when it started. Dozens of people—most of them in their teens—rushed over. Jimmy greeted each one like a lost friend. In addition to handshakes he autographed newspapers, postcards, hands, and in one case, a nose almost as long as his. About an hour later we managed to get to Brooks Brothers. The turmoil, however, didn't cease. Both dignified salesclerks and customers recognized him instantly. This time autograph signing wasn't sufficient. The audience which by now numbered more than fifty would only settle for Jimmy giving an impromptu performance. One man carrying a hand-tooled attache case said that twenty-five years before he had heard Schnozzola belt out a song about a banker who was buried with gravy on his clothes. He wished he could hear it again. For a moment, Jimmy looked perplexed. Then he smiled as he recalled the song:

This banker had gravy on his vest.
Gravy on his tie,
Gravy on his pants,
Gravy all over him.
So he went to his grave,
With gravy on his vest,
Gravy on his tie,
Gravy on his pants.
Gravy all over him.
That dirty old man!

On the taxi ride back to his hotel I commented that it was too bad he didn't have time to buy a sweater. "That's okay," he said solemnly. "I got a good look at them prices. You got to be a Rockinfellow to afford them!"

Jimmy was delighted with his new popularity, but felt that preparing for a regular TV show was too demanding. Instead he agreed to do several specials a year. Rudolf Nureyev, the Russian ballet dancer who had defected from his native country, was scheduled to appear in one of them. The State Department was very interested and dispatched a key man to do the translating. He turned out to be a Schnozzola fan. As he and Jimmy watched Nureyev spend forty-five minutes loosening up his muscles, Durante said loudly, "How about that guy? Nervy needs all that time to warm up. Me, I start cold."

Nureyev, who understood some English, pretended not to be listening. It was obvious, however, that the remark had riled him. When a reporter asked if he had ever heard of Jimmy Durante, he didn't wait for the State Department official to interpret. Immediately he replied vehemently, "*Nyet!*" Then he turned his back as Jimmy walked over to apologize. Durante was humiliated, but when he saw Nureyev leaping and pirouetting he began to applaud. He was quickly silenced by a very angry dancer. "No clapping!" Nureyev shouted.

"Nervy's right," Jimmy said. "Us artists got to work in quiet."

"Suddenly, you couldn't go into a store without seeing a picture of Jimmy and his nose," said Jackson. "They were selling Schnozzola dolls, Schnozzola yo-yo's, Schnozzola dry cereal. There was even a Schnozzola comic strip which showed him always throwing down his hat and yelling, 'Am I mortified!' When I'd kid about it he'd say, 'Don't you think Lou would be proud of the way things worked out?' "

Jimmy still made frequent appearances at nightclubs. Although his fee had increased to $10,000 a night, the routine remained pretty much the same. There was only one major change—he eliminated the Victorian etiquette book's reference to the nose being an organ that grew in size through frequent handling. Otherwise, the material was repeated. Nose gags continued to be the mainstay of his act.

Durante: I'm so dispairin' because I can't grow a mustache on my face.

Straight man: That's terrible news to hear. But why is that so?

Durante: Because it won't grow in the shade!

Durante: I've just been listed in Ripley's *Believe It or Not*.

Straight man: What did you do to rate such an honor?

Durante: I'm the only man in America who can take a shower while he's smokin' a cigar!

Durante: With this nose I can sniff out trouble even a mile away.

Straight man: What happens if the trouble is further away?

Durante: I call my cousin Willie so we can put our schnozzles together.

Straight man: And if it's further still?

Durante: I got a big family!

In September of 1955 a group of psychiatrists meeting in Los Angeles presented Jimmy with a silver plaque for bringing laughter to so many people. Dr. Henry Goldsmith was the chairman. "Never before had I experienced such frenzied jubilation," he recalled. "That room vibrated with shrieks of joy. Schnozzola's opening remarks set the stage. 'I was only five months old when I crawled to a beauty show and won first prize,' he told us. 'Ever since then the girls can't keep their hands off me.' Then he fell to his knees and stretched out his hands pleadingly as he asked us, 'Doctors, please tell me what I should do?' He was interrupted by one of my colleagues, a dignified sixty-year-old woman. 'I can see why!' she shouted as she ran up to the podium and gave him a resounding kiss. He was delighted and looked at us rougishly. 'That's exactly what I mean,' he said."

Shortly before the 1956 national election, Tennessee Senator Estes Kefauver, candidate for vice president on the Democratic ticket, gave Jimmy an elaborate coonskin cap. Durante graciously accepted the gift. "But when Senator Keyfauver ain't lookin'," Schnozzola said, "I put it away in moth balls because I'm used to my old, plain fedora hat. Besides a girl tells me it doesn't do justice to my profile."

During the late fifties, Jimmy was a steady fixture in Las Vegas's nightclubs. After each performance he would head for the gambling rooms. The casino managers tried to discourage him. Said one, "He'd put on such an impromptu show while tossing the dice that our customers stopped betting in order to watch him. We seriously considered paying Schnozzola to stay clear of the dice tables."

While in Las Vegas, Durante was interviewed for a late-night radio program. The conversation was memorable if somewhat garbled. Here are some excerpts:

Host: Schnozzola, what do you consider the most important things a person can possess?

Jimmy: Good health, workin' at somethin' you like, havin' friends you like, not hurtin' people, bein' able to buy a refrigerator. Things like that.

Host: You mentioned not hurting people.

Jimmy: By that I mean not sayin' really mean things about people an' wantin' to hurt them real bad for the sake of gettin' a laugh. An' that goes double for havin' to tell dirty jokes in your act. I've learned it ain't necessary to do that to make your audience appreciate you.

Host: That's an interesting observation. Have you always felt that way?

Jimmy: Don't get me wrong. I'm no prune. I like some of those jokes like the next guy. But there's a place an' time for tellin' them. An' also the ones you choose to tell.

Host: In the list you just gave, you included the need of having good friends. Does that include one's wife and people of the opposite sex?

Jimmy: I was married for a long time. An' to me marriage is very sacred. But let's face it. For a man it's easier to have close friends who are doin' the exact same things you are. Who are in the same business you are in. The ones you come in close contact are mainly men. You are more relaxed with people of your own sex.

Host: What is the best time of the day for you?

Jimmy: The daytime. That's when most people are up. I don't like it much when they're sleepin'.

Host: Why? Do you have trouble falling asleep?

Jimmy: It's not completely that, but I don't like wastin' my time with sleepin'.

Host: Have you ever tried reading great literature to help you fall asleep?

Jimmy: I don't have time for too much readin' heavy stuff. I wait until they're made into movies. But I've had a library card since I was a little kid.

Host: Schnozzola, what has been your life's motto? Something you always lived by?

Jimmy: Bein' good without always feelin' you have to be good.

Host: I'm not sure I know what you're saying. Please explain it.

Jimmy: There are some people who pretend they are always good like goin' to church a couple of times a day an' are sore at people who don't live like that. I've found that you don't have to be that way in order to be good.

Host: You've met a great many famous people. Who are your favorites?

Jimmy: That's a hard one to answer. If I say the wrong thing, I'll hurt their feelin's. But I'll play it safe an' say my father. In a lot of ways it's true. My father made a great impression on me for a lot of reasons.

Host: Schnozzola, what would you like to be remembered for?

Jimmy: That's easy. For makin' people laugh an' makin' them feel good.

In 1957, Durante returned briefly to the cinema where he appeared fleetingly in *Beau James*, a movie about New York City's former mayor, Jimmy Walker. Then it was back to nightclubs. Three years later he accepted a cameo role in *Pepe*, starring Cantinflas who was then the most popular comic in the Spanish speaking world. Cantinflas had recently wowed American audiences in Mike Todd's *Around the World in Eighty Days,* and Hollywood hoped to capitalize on his fame and cast him in *Pepe,* another big budget film.

"The energy of that man," said Cantinflas. "I'd be out of breath when I did a nightclub scene with him. If the director asked for a retake, Jimmy would be more than ready. He must have legs made of iron. When I complimented him about them he told me it was nothing—that his father had run backwards across the Brooklyn Bridge balancing a plate of spaghetti on his head so he could celebrate his ninetieth birthday. I'm sure Jimmy was having me on. But on second thought maybe it actually happened. With those Durantes, anything is possible."

Several months later Jimmy appeared in an Italian film *Giudizio Universale* (The Last Judgement). During the filming he was invited by one of the members of the cast to join him in seeing the sights of Rome. "Thanks for askin' me," Durante replied. "But I've already seen all of them. Back when I toured Europe in the thirties, I saw all of them sights."

"That must have required a good deal of time," the other actor said. "How long were you in Rome?"

"Nearly a whole day," Jimmy answered. "By four o'clock in the afternoon I didn't know what to do with myself!"

23

The New Mrs. Durante

On December 14, 1960, James Francis Durante and Margaret Alice Little were wed in New York City's St. Malachy Roman Catholic Church. They knelt in front of the same altar at which Schnozzola and Jeanne had made their vows thirty-nine years before. He was sixty-seven. The bride was thirty-nine.

In Damon Runyon's *Guys and Dolls*, Nathan Detroit and his Adalaide were engaged for fourteen years before saying "I do." That had been a Broadway record until Durante came along. He and Margie "went steady" for sixteen years.

"I had strong doubts about our ever being wed," Margie said. "After we had been going together for ten years, I finally took the bull by the horns. I asked him bluntly if we were going to get married. 'Married?' he answered pretending to be shocked. 'Why, we hardly know each other!'"

The lengthy courtship had been unorthodox from the beginning. The first time Durante called on her, he arrived carrying a phonograph record under his arm. He explained that one of his friends had told him that whenever a fellow did any serious wooing there should be sweet music in the background. He had come prepared.

"I was touched," Margie said. "After turning down the lamps and lighting some candles, I played Jimmy's sweet music. I was almost blasted out of my chair. It was Al Jolson singing "Swanee"—one of the loudest vocals ever!" The following Christmas, Durante presented her with a large diamond ring. "Does this mean we're formally engaged?" she asked as she started to slip it on the third finger of her left hand.

"What's the matter?" he replied teasingly. "Don't it fit on your pinky?" Several times he set wedding dates, but a few days later they were postponed. When reporters asked why he was waiting so long, they would invariably receive a flip reply:

- "Every couple needs time to learn each other's faults."
- "I used to be impulsive an' rush into things. Like the time I almost got engaged to Greta Garbo. I didn't want to lose my identity. So I managed to get out of it at the last minute. I don't want it to happen again."
- "The reason we got so many separations an' divorces is because people get married too young. That's not for me. I don't want to be no vital statistical!"

"It was touch and go all the way to the altar," Margie said. "Then one day he startled me with a change of tune. We were visiting some friends in Del Mar and the conversation centered on babies. Our friends, expecting a new arrival, were jokingly bemoaning the future—the 2:00 A.M. feedings and no more sleeping late on Sundays. 'Well, if you don't want the baby," I said, 'I'll take it.' That's when Jimmy chimed in. 'Yeah, Margie's right. We'll take it.' "Our friends reminded him that you usually have to be married before they allow you to adopt a child. 'Well, we're gonna get married, ain't we?' Jimmy asked looking at me. It was the nicest proposal I ever had."

Shortly after they were married the Durantes decided to adopt a baby. At the time, adoption was a lot easier—especially if you were a famous movie star. They selected a three-day-old infant. "We call her CeeCee," Jimmy said. "But her full name is Cecilia Alicia. The minute I saw her I knew she was the baby for us by the way she looks at my nose. Imagine, not even a week old and right away she sees my proboscitor an' begins laughin'. But the sad truth is that she, herself, got a button for a nose. I try pullin' it and gettin' the doctors to do somethin' to make it bigger. Nothin' works. So I guess Margie an' me are stuck with that little button nose."

Although Durante continued wisecracking, he was very apprehensive about the legal proceedings. He worried that the court would consider him much too old to be the father of a newborn. Holding CeeCee in his arms, Jimmy attempted to convince the judge that no heart is ever too elderly to love and care for a child. When he finished pleading his case, he thought he detected a scowl on the judge's face. "I felt I hadn't made a very convincin' argument," Durante said. "I was sure that CeeCee would be taken away from us."

His Honor, resplendent in black robe, rose from the bench, looked at Jimmy for several moments, then burst into a song Durante had made famous in his movies and nightclub act: "Fairy tales can come true. It can happen to you if you're young at heart." As the infant's godparents, Louella Parsons and Danny Thomas, cheered, the judge added, "You are exactly that, Schnozzola. The child couldn't have a better father. My best wishes to you and the new mother. Adoption approved. Case dismissed!"

Now that Jimmy had a family, Margie tried to curtail his working schedule. "That wasn't easy," said Jackson. "Clubs all over wanted him. What's more they were willing to pay extremely well. Jimmy found it hard to refuse. 'I got to take care of Margie and CeeCee,' he'd say. 'Jimmy,' I'd tell him, you've worked hard all these years. You've got enough money to sit back and relax. Why continue to knock yourself out?' "

Durante scorned the idea. "If you bug out you waste away," he replied. "It almost killed Al Jolson before that movie brought him back. I'd melt into nothin' if that phone stopped ringin'. Sure, I don't need the money, but I need the work! So it's nightclubs for me. Like they say, 'Have nose, will travel.' "

And travel he did. During the sixties he made dozens of

nightclub appearances. While performing in San Juan, Puerto Rico, Jimmy visited Muhammed Ali's training camp. He challenged the heavyweight boxer to an arm wrestling match. After several minutes of violent grunting and twitching, the contest was declared a draw. Durante appeared to be furious. "I should of been named the winner," he protested. "I didn't want to hurt him so I took it easy." Suddenly he began grimacing and holding his hand as he fell to the floor.

Ali, who was partner to this visual joke, horrified the spectators when he said, "It serves the fool right to horse around with someone as strong as me! Let the big nosed jerk lay there!"

"Muhambone," Jimmy said petulantly as he stood up and dusted himself off. "It ain't nice to call a person that!" Ali's response was to walk over to Schnozzola and kiss him on the nose.

Much as Durante mistrusted airplanes, he'd take a very early Sunday morning flight to Los Angeles in order to spend the day with Margie and CeeCee. The following morning he'd fly back. To please his daughter he interrupted his club appearances to play the part of Humpty Dumpty in a made for television special. Because of her, Jimmy also did the narration in an animated television cartoon, "Frosty the Snowman." While making it, he took time out to visit the track. One of the horses was named White Frost. Although it was a hundred to one long shot, he felt that it was a "sure perminition." White Frost came in first and Durante collected his substantial winnings. As soon as the TV film was completed he invited several hundred children to be his guests at a special showing. He gave each youngster an ice cream cone and a water pistol.

The judge who had allowed the adoption had been quite right. Schnozzola was an excellent—if somewhat overconscientious—parent. The Family Service Association named him "Concerned Father of the Year".

"Of all the honors he received," Desi Arnaz said, "That one meant the most to him. He was gaga about that child. He had been resigned to never having one and when he finally did he went overboard. Whenever CeeCee ran a slight fever or had a sleepless night, he'd start calling all the people he knew that had children of their own. Nobody was spared. He even called Dr. Benjamin Spock for some helpful ideas. Jimmy had just met the country's leading pediatrician on my television show."

Once when CeeCee developed hiccups at 11:00 P.M., Durante anxiously phoned a local physician. "I tell the doc it's an emergancy an' he has to come right over because she can't stop hiccupin'," Schnozzola said. 'Jimmy,' he tells me, 'I'm already in my pajamas gettin' ready for bed. I'm sure those hiccups will soon go away. So be patient!' That doesn't satisfy me an' I say, 'Doc, take off those pajamas an' put on your pants an' rush right over!' A few minutes later CeeCee gets over her hiccups. So I call him back. Lucky, he's still there. 'Doc,' I say. 'Take off the pants an' put back on the pajamas.'

"The things us parents have to go through to raise a kid healthy!"

Other than his wife and daughter, the only pastime Schnozzola enjoyed was handicapping the horses. His strategy was to bet on five or six horses competing in the same race. At the track he was often heard shouting, "C'mon everybody!" When CeeCee developed a love of horses he bought her a pony of her own. "She's a chip off this old brick," he'd say proudly.

The Durantes had two houses in California—Beverly Hills and Del Mar. By celebrity standards they were comparatively simple places. "But I have two swimmin' pools," he'd brag. "One for swimmin' an' the other for rinsin' off." Drivers of sightseeing buses loved to pull up in front of Jimmy's Beverly Hills' house because they knew they'd always receive a warm welcome. Unlike most of the other celebrities whose homes were part of the star tour, Schnozzola looked forward to their arrival. The moment he spotted one, he'd bolt out and shout, "Glad you folks stopped by."

Frank Ellis, a veteran bus operator, recalled those visits. "The way he greeted us made you feel that he was really glad we'd come," Ellis said. "On a particularly hot day he'd appear wearing swimming trunks and a checked kerchief tied around his head. He'd be carrying some glasses and a pitcher of lemonade. 'A penny a glass!' he'd yell. But you knew he wasn't selling—it was his way of letting us know he was glad we were there. On Christmas he'd hand out big, black cigars to everybody. Even the ladies. He was the direct opposite of W. C. Fields who would lie in wait for us and aim his BB gun at any passenger who dared to stare."

Whenever the Durante family went to New York City, they would stay at a hotel close to Broadway. "The reason is plain an' simple,' Jimmy explained. "When the taxicabs start bangin' into each other an' the crowd starts yellin', the sweet music they make helps put little CeeCee to sleep. I've been all around this country and nothin' compares to the air an' smell of Broadway."

He was performing at the Copacabana in the winter of 1961 when he was summoned by MGM. They wanted to cast him in *Jumbo*, a filmed re-creation of Billy Rose's musical that Jimmy had starred in twenty-six years before. At first he was reluctant to repeat the role. But when he learned that MGM planned on making it a "high-class blocksmasher" and that Doris Day, Martha Raye, and Stephen Boyd were also in it, he changed his mind. "I figure those kids need a mature person like me," he said.

The film had its premiere in the Christmas show attraction at New York's Radio City Music Hall. Usually, motion picture attenders start exiting the moment the movie ends. Not this time. As soon as the curtain dropped, the entire audience rose to give the film a standing ovation. For several minutes there was loud applause and shrieks of, "Bravo, Schnozzola!"

Jimmy's last screen appearance was in 1963 in Stanley Kramer's *It's A Mad Mad Mad Mad World*. Kramer had secured the services of many of the best known comedians in show business. Entertainers like Durante, Milton Berle, Sid Caesar, Buster Keaton, Terry-Thomas, Andy Devine, Joe E. Brown, Mickey Rooney, Buddy Hackett, Don Knotts, Ben Blue, Eddie "Rochester" Anderson, Edward Everett Horton, Carl Reiner, Dick Shawn, the Three Stooges, Jonathan

Winters, and Phil Silvers. When the movie was completed, the cast was asked to name the comic they regarded as the funniest.

"Naturally our first choice was ourselves," said Phil Silvers. "But after that initial pick, the only one we all could agree on was Schnozzola. As he got older his timing had become superb. He had learned to milk a scene for all its worth, then stop and milk it some more. What he did may look easy, but you try doing it. You can steal his jokes, but not his delivery."

John Kennedy was another Durante fan. At White House parties, the President often attempted a Schnozzola imitation. "To be told that he did it well," said Jacqueline Kennedy Onassis, "was a compliment he relished. I believe it was a mutual admiration society. When Jack was assassinated, Schnozzola sent me a very warm message."

"Kennedy's impersonation may have been good," said the future president Ronald Reagan. "But I'm sure it couldn't compare with mine. My Durante specialty was to shake my head and shout, 'Hot-cha-cha' several times. I'd do it so vigorously that more than once I slipped on the carpet and landed on my butt."

In September of 1964, Jimmy was feted for his fifty years in show business—actually he had been performing for fifty-four years. The long overdue dinner was held at the Hollywood Roosevelt Hotel. Hundreds of his friends attended. Among them: Bob Hope, George Burns, Gene Kelly, Eddie Jackson, Tallulah Bankhead, Desi Arnaz, Sophie Tucker, Lauritz Melchior, George Raft, and Walter Winchell.

President Lyndon Johnson and Republican leader Barry Goldwater sent telegrams. Former President Harry Truman wrote, "I was rather surprised to learn that it is only your fiftieth year in show business. I had the impression that you've been around for at least a hundred years bringing pleasure and happiness to thousands and thousands of people. I, for one, hope you go on forever."

One of the messages Durante was proudest of came from Nelson Rockefeller, who at the time was governor of New York State. "I'm donating fifty thousand dollars in your name to charity," Rockefeller had written. "A thousand dollars for each year you've brought such gladness to the American people."

Upon receipt of the letter, Jimmy was momentarily speechless. He recovered quickly and said, "That Rockinfellow may be a financial typhoon, but one with a golden heart."

24

Still Young at Heart

In his older years Schnozzola admitted that his eyesight was no longer perfect, yet he scorned wearing glasses. "It's not that I'm a vanity," he explained. "I just don't like puttin' specs on my face because everybody looks a whole lot better to me if I don't." Grudgingly, he agreed to wear them when in 1967 he approved a television deal that guaranteed him $12,500 a week to costar with the Lennon Sisters, a popular singing group. As he signed the contract he said, "Now maybe I can read the sign that says the gents room. You got to stop makin' those letters smaller an' smaller!"

The Lennon Sisters had been headliners on "The Lawrence Welk Show" which had earned them a large and dedicated following of adults and teenagers. That was noteworthy since a recent nationwide survey revealed that few weekly television series appealed to both parent and child. Anxious to bridge the generation gap, ABC-TV decided that by bringing the Lennons together with Durante the show would draw both young and old viewers. The show was called "Jimmy Durante Presents the Lennon Sisters."

It was suggested that several wounded soldiers, who had just returned from Vietnam, should be featured on each program. Jimmy objected. "Those poor kids saw enough trouble already," he said sorrowfully. "I was warned to be careful about signin'. But it was much too much money to turn away from. Maybe it was a mistake my goin' ahead? Here I was workin' the clubs, doin' guest shots when I felt like, an' takin' care of our little CeeCee. An' what happens? I'm all of a sudden workin' with those wonnerful Lennon Sisters every week an' makin' a king's random."

He should have known better when he saw some of the preliminary scripts. They called for him to be known as "Electric Nose of the Rock World." To make it look authentic he'd be decked out in a jet black wig and long sideburns. The Lennons would appear as "The Four Hankies."

"This improbable combination was responsible for some of the most absurd moments in television," said Joe Franklin, who for years has conducted a radio program devoted to entertainment world nostalgia. "It's difficult to understand why it failed to click. The idea was not bad—a first-class comedian in his seventies and four top-notch young, pretty singers. Ordinarily, you could team Jimmy up with King Kong and the performance would sparkle. But I'm afraid this was an exception. Too often it lacked taste and seemed lifeless. They tried saving it by bringing in name guests like Bob Hope and Phyllis Diller. It didn't help much."

Franklin felt that old age had finally caught up with Durante. A few weeks after the show was canceled, he caught Jimmy's act in a New York nightclub. Before Jimmy started performing, Franklin went backstage to interview him for his program, "Memory Lane." He vividly recalled the visit. "I was talking to an old man," he said. "Schnozzola had deep wrinkles all over his face, the few remaining hairs on his head were snow white. He appeared to be sluggish as he attempted to answer my questions."

Feeling very upset, Franklin returned to his seat. A few minutes later he watched Jimmy dash out to the raised stage. The "old man" had suddenly become a bundle of exuberant energy. With his ragged fedora jauntily cocked over one eye he started throwing sheet music around. Sitting sidesaddle on his piano stool he scowled at the clarinetist and accused him of playing with only one lip. "I'm surrounded by assassins," he shouted. Pretending to be enraged he tossed out his opening gag.

Durante: Comin' here I had to walk in the middle of the gutter.
Straight man: Why, Schnozzola?
Durante: Because of the fact that I owe money to people on both of the sidewalks. This way I keep them from givin' me the kiss of debt!

"Everyone in the audience roared," Franklin said. "I was the loudest. Schnozzola, who had survived Prohibition, the Depression, the switch from vaudeville to movies to radio to television, was still the dynamic Mr. Malaprop I had always admired. Later I related the story on my program and received dozens of approving letters. Some from really big names. In a business where bitter rivalries are everyday affairs, this remarkable man had managed to have but one enemy—the King's English!"

Jimmy's English stayed happily a mixture of Lower East Side and Coney Island American. His writers were under strict orders to avoid doctoring up any multisyllable words that appeared in the scripts. "We were warned to let him do the mixing-up himself," said Bernie Lewis who worked on many of Durante's TV specials. "However, I don't think it was intentional—he just saw words differently. I once asked him about his errors of tongue. 'If I'd gone more to school,' he replied thoughtfully, 'I could pronounce those big words by now. An' then where would I be? I'll tell you. Washin' dishes. That's where! People would still be laughin' at me but I wouldn't get paid so much.' A moment later he ceased being so long-faced and added with mock solemnity, 'I'm really a man of letters. A and B!' "

Durante would be handed a script that contained the word *corpuscle*, and out would come *corkpuckle; exuberant* would be *exubilant; catastrophe—catostroke*. When he went out to buy a blue cheviot suit, he asked for one made of chevrolet

166

material. His misspeaking flair was evident in conversations with two equally adroit malaprop artists. They occurred at a dinner that honored outstanding figures in baseball. Jimmy was the master of ceremonies.

With baseball pitcher Dizzy Dean

Durante: People are forever pickin' on the way I talk.

Dean: Pardner, the same thing happened to me when I said, "The player slud into first base." But pretty soon if you don't let it worry you too much it goes plump away.

Durante: That's mighty good advice you just gave, tellin' me not to worry. It gives me a piece of mind.

Dean: That's important to have in this modern world. Sometimes it spins around so fast, it's even faster than my fastest pitch used to be.

Durante: You know Diz I always wanted to be an outstandin' pitcher just like you are to the fans.

Dean: I appreciate your comment. But did you say them flattering words because you wanted a favor from me?

Durante: No, Diz. There was no exterior motive in why I said them. I really mean it from the top of my heart. You've always been the apple in my eye.

With baseball manager Casey Stengel

Durante: Casey what do you really say when you pramulate up to the pitcher's mount?

Stengel: Schnozz, that's an invisable secret between him and me and even a stack of Bibles wouldn't drag it out of me.

Durante: Aw, Casey, you can confine in me. Every Tom, Dick an' Dora knows my lips are sealed tight when it comes to private particulars.

Casey: Well if you promise on your word of honor. Yesterday for instance, I told a name I can't divulge in order to steady him down from being wild to the other side, I took a 10 and ½ size shoe.

Durante: Casey, my nose is about that exact same size.

New York's Cardinal Spellman had been a guest at the baseball dinner. A few weeks later he presented the Catholic Youth Organization's gold medal to Durante for the "Innocent and unsophisticated way of expressing yourself." Handing the award to Jimmy, the Cardinal said, "Schnozzola, you possess the wonderful naivety of a young, trusting child. No matter how old you get, don't ever lose it!"

Not only was Schnozzola's language unique, but his songs were equally distinguished. They included: "Who Will Be with Me When I'm Far Away in Far Rockaway?"; "Did You Ever Have the Feeling That You Wanted to Go, *Still* You Wanted to Stay?"; "So I Ups to Him, An' He Ups to Me"; "A Dissa an' a Datta."

"Schnozzola and I worked for the same cabaret a long time ago," said Irving Berlin who had composed hundreds of songs. "I hope that some of mine made sense. None of Jimmy's did. They were filled with the most wonderful nonsense. One of my great pleasures was hearing him sing, "I Can Do Without Broadway, but Can Broadway Do Without Me?" The answer to that title is very simple, 'NO!' When you say Jimmy's songs are unusual, it's an understatement. They are out of this world."

Goodnight, Mr. D.

The last years of Durante's life were filled with a mixture of profound grief and prideful happiness. The sorrow was brought on by a series of strokes which prevented him from bringing laughter to his devoted fans. The blissfulness stemmed from having a wife and daughter who idolized him. "All the time my Margie an' CeeCee let me know how they feel about me," he told Desi Arnaz. "You'd think I was some kind of Clark Gable with Rockinfellow's money the way they keep treatin' me."

In 1968 Margie gave him an elaborate surprise party for his seventy-fifth birthday. It was so lavish that Milton Berle, one of the guests, remarked, "No expense was spared. In all my days I've never seen anything to compare. It was so lush that even the dust was sterling silver!"

The cake was in the shape of a piano—4 feet 7 inches tall and 5 feet 3 inches wide. It had taken the pastry chefs four days of around-the-clock labor to create the work of art. They used 240 pounds of flour, 20 crates of eggs, 180 pounds of sugar, 50 pounds of butter. The masterpiece was topped with 200 pounds of frosting. A chocolate-covered stool stood in front of the edible piano.

The highpoint of the evening was when seven-year-old CeeCee popped out of the cake and jumped into Jimmy's arms. "You thought I was home in bed, didn't you Daddy?" she said. A very startled Schnozzola kissed his daughter as he reached for a handkerchief to wipe away tears. The following week however, he returned to his "reduced" schedule: performances in a Las Vegas nightclub; taping a TV special; recording a record album entitled *Songs for Sunday*; agreeing to be honorary mayor of Del Mar.

Doctors felt that his frenzied pace may have contributed to his physical decline. His initial stroke in November of 1972 left him partially paralyzed. The once powerful voice was reduced to a weak murmur. The eighty-year-old comedian had been scheduled to appear in Miami Beach. "I'm very sorry not to be able to make it," he wired the management. "Be sure to give the folks my embarrassment." He vowed that he'd soon return to show business. But at the end of the year his doctors told him that it was a hopeless dream. Sadly, he announced his retirement.

"For someone who had always been very active that was almost an impossible task," said Desi Arnaz, who visited him frequently. "He'd struggle against being an invalid. There he'd be sitting in his wheelchair wearing that blue terry cloth bathrobe he refused to get rid of. He'd be reading the *Racing Form* still doping out the ponies. Suddenly, he'd turn to me and whisper, 'Desi, I got a sure thing for you in the second race. Number 7, 16, 19, 23 and 31!' When I'd look concerned about his deteriorating condition, he'd try to comfort me. 'I'm feelin' better,' he'd say in a very weak tone. 'It's slow, but don't forget it takes a lot of strength to support a nose like mine.' Then he'd proudly show me the latest blue ribbon his daughter had won."

CeeCee is an excellent equestrian and received numerous awards attesting to her riding skill. "That kid knows more about horses than me an' you put together," he once told Arnaz. "She's a regular cowboy on a horse. Even more then Gene Autry."

Durante and Arnaz had been friends for many years. Jimmy's illness drew them even closer. Arnaz attempted to explain their association. "I think part of the reason I'd visit him so often," he said, "was because he made me realize what really counted in life—being yourself. He was always natural—never putting on airs. I'm probably saying this badly, but what I mean is that Jimmy was always himself. And he made everybody want to act the same way."

Danny Thomas, another steady visitor, seemed to agree. "There was something about the Schnozzola that brought out the best in you," he said. "It was almost as if he challenged you to put your best foot forward. I've given a good deal of thought as to why it was so. I think I now have the answer. It's because Schnozzola wasn't a phony. So you were never one in his presence."

In 1972, pale, tremendously underweight, and confined to a wheelchair, he was one of the few big names to attend the Damon Runyon Cancer Fund Dinner at New York's Waldorf Astoria on the occasion of its twenty-fifth anniversary. Most of the other celebrities who had been invited said they were too busy to make the scene. "I was surprised he'd made that cross-country trip in the condition he was in," said Arnaz. "But then I should have realized he'd be there. Jimmy just couldn't refuse anybody. He was the easiest touch I've ever known."

Some months later Schnozzola again visited New York. This time he was the guest of honor at the thirty-ninth annual luncheon of the American Newspaper Publishers Association. The 1,800 guests gave him a standing ovation as Margie wheeled him to the head table. He tried to acknowledge the cheering by rising. Realizing that he couldn't, he waved. After a series of tributes, William Randolph Hearst, Jr., the chairman, handed him a golden statuette. "Thanks," Schnozzola mumbled. Then, as his wife leaned close to him, he seemed to draw new strength. He reached for a table microphone and slowly sang, "Inka Dinka Doo."

When in June of 1975 CeeCee graduated from twelfth grade, he and Margie invited their daughter's classmates and parents to a dinner party at the Beverly Hills home. Jimmy, seated in his wheelchair, looked on proudly as CeeCee and her young friends splashed each other in the swimming pool. The last stroke had affected his speech so much that it was very difficult to comprehend what he was saying. However, he managed to make himself understood. He whispered to Desi Arnaz, "I have only one wish—to live long enough to go to CeeCee's wedding."

It was not to be. Although Jimmy lived for five more years he was in and out of hospitals. For his eighty-third birthday nearly a thousand people filled the banquet hall at the Beverly Hilton Hotel. Danny Thomas and Robert Alda were the masters of ceremonies. Lights were dimmed as Jimmy was wheeled in. The guests lit matches in the darkened room and sang "Happy Birthday." That seemed to be a challenge to him. Once again he attempted to sing "Inka Dinka Doo." The song was inaudible but the event did raise more than $100,000 for the Jimmy Durante Pavilion of the Villa Scabrini Home for the Aged.

In May of 1979 he was hospitalized for several weeks with an upper respiratory infection. Carlos Gonzales, an orderly, said, "Sick as he was, he kept making faces to get me to laugh. Once he tried to balance a glass of water on his nose but it fell off and made him all wet. He just smiled. I cried inside."

On January 9, 1980, Jimmy returned to the hospital. The doctors told Margie that he had pneumonitis.* His condition took a turn for the worse as he remained in a state of semi-consciousness. Suffering from lung congestion, he died on the morning of January twenty-ninth at the age of eighty-six.

Margie and CeeCee† were joined by hundreds of worshippers who attended the service at Beverly Hills' Good Shepherd Church. Hundreds more had to be turned away for lack of space. Actor Marlon Brando managed to squeeze into a back pew. It was the first time he had ever been seen at a Hollywood funeral. When a reporter asked him why he had

---

*"We received hundreds of calls inquiring about Schnozzola's condition," said Myrna Effron, a hospital employee. "The most persistent ones came from Eddie Jackson." Jimmy's old friend was too ill to visit him. He died nine months later.

†CeeCee, still an ardent horsewoman, was married last year. Her mother continues to live in Del Mar where she is affectionately known as Mrs. Schnozzola.

come, he replied, "To pay tribute to a man who taught me how to laugh."

The casket was covered with red roses and his battered fedora. Bob Hope and Danny Thomas led the tribute. Hope said, "If success is measured by the number of friends you have, believe me, Jimmy Durante was the most successful man I know of."

"We love you, Schnozzola," Thomas finished. "This is not a eulogy but a love letter because the sweetest, gentlest, most generous and talented man I have ever known has left us."

Epilogue

While researching this book I discovered that people who came in close contact with Durante had favorite Schnozzola anecdotes they insisted on telling over and over. Broadway producer Billy Rose enjoyed hearing them so much that he often included "Unforgettable Schnozzola Yarns" in his annual Christmas letter.

Bob Hope was another collector of Durante tales. "After I listened to Jimmy's latest misadventure," he said, "I'd find myself still laughing days later. Sometimes right in the middle of Hollywood Boulevard and Vine. Once when I told him that he was a menace to safe driving, he looked at me innocently. 'Bob,' he replied, 'if that bein' the case, I promise from now on I'll keep my mouth shut tight!' "

Fortunately, he didn't. Here is a sample of "Unforgettable Schnozzola Yarns." I think you'll agree that most of them are hilarious, some poignant, and a few downright bizarre.

George Burns:

"One beautiful afternoon Jimmy and Eddie Cantor were at the Del Mar racetrack. They ran into a horse owner they knew from Louisville, Kentucky. He gave them a tip on the first race. On such good advice Jimmy and Eddie bet $100. The horse won. It paid twenty to one. That was just the beginning. Those two didn't lose another race that afternoon. It didn't matter which horse they bet—be it a favorite, or a long shot—the horse they picked always won. On that day, they were touched by magic. After they cashed in six straight winning tickets, Jimmy looked at Eddie and said seriously, 'You gotta promise me one thing. No matter what happens in the next race, we go back to show business!' "

Shirley Temple:

"I had just finished filming *Little Miss Broadway* [1938] with him. To celebrate, the studio had arranged a gala party. Eleanor Roosevelt, wife of President Franklin D. Roosevelt, was the guest of honor. She had been shown a preview of the movie. Graciously, she complimented every one in the cast on having done an excellent job. When the band started playing, Schnozzola bowed and invited Mrs. Roosevelt to dance with him. She was wearing flat heels but still towered over him. They were a sight to behold. As they tangoed past me I heard Jimmy saying, 'Mrs. R., please don't tell the President about us. It'll just make him jealous!' "

Richard Maney:

"As a theatrical press agent I've clashed the cymbals for hundreds of Broadway shows. In my capacity of trying to make clients look respectable I've had to visit their dressing rooms. None were comparable to the gentleman of the long nose. His dressing room was a composite of a bus terminal, an all-night cafeteria, and an Elk's lodge meeting. Many of Jimmy's callers were policemen in search of a quick one, retired waiters, vaudeville performers, messengers, unemployed bit players, and others seeking a haven or a fast buck.

"One evening his dressing room was more crowded than usual. It was Halloween night and kids from the neighborhood were lined up in front of a table where Jimmy was holding court. He was supposed to be a fortune teller but for some strange reason he was wearing an Indian feather headdress. There was a large crystal ball in front of him. He waved his hands over it and every time a kid came by he'd say very slowly, 'You ... will ... soon ... come ... into ... a ... fortune!' Then with an elegant flourish he handed the youngster a shiny silver dollar.

"Another time Jimmy was chewed out for allowing a Bowery bum to use his dressing room for sleeping quarters. Schnozzola had a ready scrambled reply. 'That there man is a real gentleman,' Jimmy explained. 'He's very careful when he strikes a match on the furniture that it's always with the grain.'"

Ethel Merman:

"I'll never forget our tryout in Boston for *Red, Hot and Blue!* [1936]. We were both sharing the lead and naturally concerned about each other. Often, Jimmy wouldn't show until minutes before the curtain went up. One evening just before we went on I was told that Schnozz had come down with a very sore throat and was unable to speak. I ran over to his dressing room. When I knocked, a very hoarse voice croaked, 'Come on in an' look at an almost dead body!' There he was, lying down with a scarf wrapped tightly around his throat, smoking a big, fat cigar. PS: That night he got about a dozen curtain calls."

Ed Sullivan:

"During the Second World War, Father Delany, the chaplain at Staten Island's Halloran General Hospital, called me. He said that he had just read Jimmy Durante was in town and could I get him to perform for the soldiers on the following day. I phoned Jimmy at the Hotel Astor and discovered he had a bad cold and was scheduled to give a radio show the next day. But to my surprise he agreed. We worked out a precise schedule to get him to the broadcast which involved his catching a particular ferry.

"The soldiers who were there included a shipload of wounded men who had been prisoners of war. When I introduced Jimmy, the crowd went wild. He did his routine and the applause was even louder. Then instead of leaving he did another number, then a third and a fourth. Reluctantly, he left the stage when I introduced the next act. 'Are you out of your mind?' I said to him backstage. 'You'll never make your broadcast!' That was when he told me to look in the front row. I did.

" 'Ed,' he said. 'Now you can see why I stayed. When I saw that I realized that my broadcast wasn't so important.

"Sitting in the front row were two young lieutenants who had each lost an arm and were applauding by clapping their two remaining hands together."

Marlene Dietrich:

"Jimmy was instrumental in the sale of thousands of dollars of war bonds. He frequently accompanied me on fund-raising tours. Once we were appearing together at a Los Angeles rally where everyone seemed to be sitting on their hands. Sales were practically nonexistent. That's when he said to me, 'Don't worry, Marlene. I'll soon fix it.' With that he told the crowd, 'For all of you who buy bonds, Marlene an' me will wash all the windows in your house free of charge!' Suddenly, there was a great deal of activity. For the next few weeks we did exactly what Jimmy had promised. I've still got a sore back to prove it!"

A. E. Hotchner:

"At the time I was writing an article for *Cosmopolitan* magazine and had come to interview him in his suite at the Hotel Astor. As I walked in, I found him on his hands and knees about to crawl under the bed. 'I'm searchin' for my eyeglasses,' he explained. 'Oh, the last time I saw them they were in the refrigerator,' said Eddie Jackson, who was also in the room. Jimmy nodded as if the reply made good sense. When he noticed my bewilderment, he attempted to make every-

177

thing clear. 'For years all I ate for breakfast was two raw eggs,' Jimmy said. 'Then one mornin' I try yogurt. I sample a mouthful an' spit it in the sink. But finally it gets to me. Now yogurt's incontestable as raw eggs. So that's why my eyeglasses was in the ice box. See?' "

Robert Benchley:

"One night I visited the Copacabana. I had brought along my good friend Dashiell Hammett. A cheer went up when Schnozzola started performing. As usual there was a fine madness to his satire. After he finished, he walked over to our table. 'Mr. Dashiell Hammett is a world famous author,' I said as I introduced my guest. I commented on their resemblance—that they both possessed protracted protuberances. Jimmy appeared to be furious at what I'd said.

" 'Nobody looks like Durante!' he yelled. 'Nobody!' I started to beg forgiveness, but before I could utter three words, he said, 'It ain't nice to insult someone so distinguishable like Mr. Dashboard Hammer.' "

Roy Campanella:

"I never actually knew if Schnozzola was a Brooklyn Dodger fan or rooted for the New York Yankees. But I'll say this for him, he loved baseball games no matter what. When he'd come to Ebbet's Field, he'd always sit behind home plate and carefully watch me catch. He'd shout instructions, 'Cantorbella, keep yer glove up higher!' Or 'Cantorbella, you should move back two inches!' I told him that my correct name was Campanella. He answered, 'Isn't that what I just said, Cantorbella.'

"The first time I saw him was right after I was brought up by the Dodgers. A man sitting behind him started razzing me because I was black. He'd shout things like, 'If this keeps up, soon the entire team won't be needing sun lamps!' Most of the insults were lots worse. Schnozzola could see how upset I was. He turned to this guy and said something. It must have been quite a mouthful because the man shut up immediately.

I didn't have a chance to thank Schnozzola until a few months later when my wife and I caught his act in some cabaret. 'It ain't fair to judge a man by what color he is,' he said. 'But Cantorbella, if you want to remain in the major leagues you should start swingin' yer bat a little earlier!' "

Steve Allen:

"One day in 1949, still new at the comedy dodge, I walked off the stage at the Hollywood Bowl where I had been a small part of a huge benefit. Unnoticed by a score of photographers who were clustered around the just-arrived Durante, I was about to leave. Suddenly, Schnozzola's voice boomed out, 'Hey Steve, get into this thing with me.' He reached, pulled me close and put an arm around me, so that my picture, too, was taken by all those otherwise uninterested photographers. When I tried to thank him, he pretended to be cross. 'How do you like that?' he said. 'Everybody wantsa get into the act!' "

Clifton Fadiman:

"I was the moderator of the television show, 'Information Please.' Our panel was supposed to guess the identity of the mystery guest. They were blindfolded. After asking several questions they shouted out, 'Schnozzola!' They had guessed so quickly that we had loads of extra time. That was when I said, 'Jimmy, can you touch your scapula with your patella?' I wasn't prepared for his worried reply: 'I hope that the program ain't gettin' off-color!' "

Bennett Cerf:

"I'll never forget a duet that featured Professor Albert Einstein playing the violin and Maestro Jimmy Durante at the piano. The two men had volunteered their musical talent for a heart fund raising show. 'I don't play classical so good,' said Schnozzola when they finished approximately in unison. 'But that Professor Einstein makes even more mistakes then me. I don't think he can count so good.' "

Lucille Ball:

"I once co-starred with Jimmy in the Los Angeles Memorial Coliseum. I was riding a horse named Bessie. Suddenly, my pants which were skintight started to rip—you know just where. When I came to a stop, Jimmy could tell how embarrassed I was. I whispered what had happened. He listened and gave me a great idea. He said that I should tell the audience that if I got off the horse, they'd have a free show because of my busted britches. That's exactly what I said. It got the biggest laugh of the night. Then bless his heart, he held out a large beach towel for me. I'll never know where he got it. All I know is that he saved me having a real 'catostroke!' "

Martha Raye:

"In 1965, Jimmy and I were asked to present the documentary Oscar at the Academy Awards ceremony that was being held in the Santa Monica Auditorium. As the orchestra began playing 'Hello, Young Lovers,' we marched on to the stage. The winner was a documentary that had been made by the U.S. Information Agency. Four young men with long flowing locks came forward to claim their Oscars. Jimmy took one look at them and patted his own bald head. Then he whispered in a tone that could be heard in the last row, 'Martha, look at the hair on these guys!' The audience broke up. Earlier, Jimmy had told me to act dignified like him."

Hubert H. Humphrey:

"In '68 when I was running for the Presidency, we held a rally for New Jersey senior citizens. Jimmy Durante was asked to entertain. At the time he was seventy-five years old, but acted more like a teenager. He didn't walk, he bounced. I think of myself as being energetic. Well, compared to him I was long over the hill. The crowd started laughing the moment he told them that he had been born on New York City's Lower East

Side where everybody had to be a Democrat. 'Once after an election,' he said, 'two Republican votes turned up. A special investigation was called to investigate.' That put the audience in such a happy mood that he zoomed in with another joke: His seven-year-old daughter threatened to pull off his nose. 'Daddy,' she said, 'without it you won't be famous anymore.' Then Schnozzola winked at the audience and added slyly, 'I wasn't taken' no chances so I raised her allowance!'

"Later, I sent him a thank-you note. Back came a telephone call: 'When you get elected, there's one thing I want—an invitation to the White House so I can sleep in Abraham Lincoln's bed.' I ran into him shortly after my defeat. 'I was only kiddin' about that Lincoln thing,' he said, trying to cheer me up. 'I hear Abe's mattress ain't so soft no more!' "

Readers may accuse me of being too partisan. I think not. It's simply that I was writing about a very decent and loveable man. I'm reminded of something Dr. Henry Goldsmith told me. Goldsmith is the Los Angeles psychiatrist who had presented a silver plaque to Durante for making people feel happy.

"During the award ceremony," Dr. Goldsmith said, "I sat next to him on the dais and we engaged in a long conversation. Throughout the meal he seemed to be at ease, especially when someone requested his autograph. Then he'd rise, make an awkward bow, and oblige with his childish scrawl. To one guest who thanked him for providing so much pleasure, he remarked, 'By rights, you should be the one to get the thanks for takin' the trouble to watch me. After all, the only thing I do is pokin' fun at my nose. An' that ain't hard to do.' When our waiter stopped to shake his hand, Jimmy said, 'Now that I finally got your attention, the least you can do is fill my water glass.' Quickly he added, 'I'm just kiddin'. To protect my health I drink only imported seltzer.'

"I came to the conclusion that Durante wasn't a very complicated man. Quite the contrary. I'd label him as being a very naive person who really believed that all people are basically decent. And they were—to him. I discovered that his constant use of ungrammatical speech wasn't an act. He may not have been schooled enough to use proper language, but he certainly was highly intuitive. Wise enough to know what people wanted—talented enough to give it to them. The Pagliacci theory that all clowns are laughing on the outside while crying within, doesn't seem to apply to him. I'd say that Schnozzola enjoyed being Schnozzola. He also enjoyed his audience. They could tell that the moment he opened his mouth. That may be why he had so many devoted fans."

I admit to being one of them. Over the years I've written about numerous show business personalities—it was rare not to run into detractors. In Durante's case I couldn't find any—not that I didn't try. Although I must have talked to several hundred people, I couldn't locate any Schnozzola fault finders. Instead, they all seemed to agree with a description Bob Hope had tagged on Jimmy: "To know him was to love him. And to love him made your sides split with laughter."

Jimmy Durante well deserved all the praise he received. Success could not have happened to a nicer person.

—JHAN ROBBINS
Columbia, South Carolina

FILMS OF JIMMY DURANTE

Roadhouse Nights (1930—Paramount)

New Adventures of Get-Rich-Quick Wallingford (1931–MGM)

The Cuban Love Song (1931—MGM)

The Passionate Plumber (1932—MGM)

The Wet Parade (1932—MGM)

Speak Easily (1932—MGM)

Blondie of the Follies (1932—MGM)

The Phantom President (1932—Paramount)

What! No Beer? (1933—MGM)

Hell Below (1933—MGM)

Broadway to Hollywood (1933—MGM)

Meet the Baron (1933—MGM)

Palooka (1934—United Artists)

George White's Scandals (1934—Fox)

Hollywood Party (1934—MGM)

Strictly Dynamite (1934—RKO)

Student Tour (1934—MGM)

Carnival (1935—Columbia)

Land Without Music (1936—British)

Sally, Irene and Mary (1938—20th Century-Fox)

Start Cheering (1938—Columbia)

Little Miss Broadway (1938—20th Century-Fox)

Melody Ranch (1940—Republic)

You're in the Army Now (1941—Warner Brothers)

The Man Who Came to Dinner (1942—Warner Brothers)

Two Girls and a Sailor (1944—MGM)

Music for Millions (1945—MGM)

Two Sisters from Boston (1946—MGM)

It Happened in Brooklyn (1947—MGM)

This Time for Keeps (1947—MGM)

On an Island with You (1948—MGM)

The Great Rupert (1950—Eagle Lion)

The Milkman (1950—Universal)

Beau James (1957—Paramount) (unbilled cameo)

Pepe (1960—Columbia)

The Last Judgement (1961—Italian)

Jumbo (1962—MGM)

It's a Mad, Mad, Mad, Mad World (1963—United Artists)

SHOWS OF JIMMY DURANTE

Show Girl (1929)
The New Yorkers (1930)
Strike Me Pink (1933)
Jumbo (1935)
Red, Hot and Blue! (1936)
Stars in Your Eyes (1939)
Keep Off the Grass (1940)

BIBLIOGRAPHY

Adler, Irene. *I Remember Jimmy: The Life & Times of Jimmy Durante.* Arlington House: Westport, Connecticut, 1980.

Asbury, Herbert. *The Great Illusion: An Informal History of Prohibition.* Doubleday: New York, 1950.

Astaire, Fred. *Steps in Time.* Harper & Brothers: New York, 1959.

Atkinson, Brooks. *Broadway.* Macmillan: New York, 1970.

Barton, Jack. *Blue Book of Tin Pan Alley.* Century House: New York, 1950.

Bergreen, Laurence. *As Thousands Cheer* (Irving Berlin). Viking: New York, 1990.

Berle, Milton. *B.S. I Love You.* McGraw-Hill: New York, 1988.

Blesh, Rudi and Harriet Janis. *They All Played Ragtime.* Grove Press: New York, 1950.

Botkin, B. A., editor. *New York City Folklore.* Random House: New York, 1956.

Burns, George with David Fisher. *All My Best Friends.* Putnam: New York, 1989.

Cahn, William. *The Laugh Makers.* Bramwell House: New York, 1957.

_____*Good Night, Mrs. Calabash.* Duell, Sloan and Pearce: New York, 1963.

Cantor, Eddie with Jane Lesner Ardmore. *Take My Life*. Doubleday: New York, 1957.

Cohan, George M. *Twenty Years on Broadway & the Years It Took to Get There: The True Story of a Trouper's Life from the Cradle to the Closed Shop*. Harper & Brothers: New York, 1924.

Crowther, Bosley. *Hollywood Rajah* (Lewis B. Mayer). Holt, Rinehart and Winston: New York, 1960.

Davidson, Marshall. *Life in America* (volume II). Houghton Mifflin: Boston, 1951.

Durante, Jimmy and J. C. Kofoed. *Night Clubs*. Knopf: New York, 1931.

Einstein, Izzy. *Prohibition Agent No. 1*. Frederick A. Stokes: New York, 1932.

Fowler, Gene. *Schnozzola*. Viking: New York, 1951.

Friedrich, Otto. *City of Nets: A Portrait of Hollywood in the 1940's*. Harper & Row: New York, 1986.

Gaver, Jack. *There's Laughter in the Air*. Greenberg: New York, 1945.

Goodman, Ezra. *The Fifty Year Decline and Fall of Hollywood*. Simon and Schuster: New York, 1961.

Green, Abel, editor. *The Spice of Variety*. Henry Holt: New York, 1952.

Hecht, Ben. *A Child of the Century*. Simon and Schuster: New York, 1954.

Hindus, Milton. *The Old East Side*. Jewish Publication Society: Philadelphia, 1969.

Hope, Bob with Pete Martin. *Have Tux, Will Travel*. Simon and Schuster: New York, 1954.

Jessel, George. *Elegy in Manhattan*. Holt, Rinehart and Winston: New York, 1961.

Kasson, John. *Amusing the Million: Coney Island at the Turn of the Century*. Hill and Wang: New York, 1978.

Kobler, John. *Capone*. G. P. Putnam's Sons: New York, 1971.

Lauder, Sir Harry. *Roamin' in the Gloamin'*. J. P. Lippincott, London, 1928.

Laurie, Joe. *Vaudeville: From the Honky-Tonks to the Palace*. Henry Holt: New York, 1953.

Lee, Peggy. *An Autobiography*. Donald I Fine: New York, 1989.

Maney, Richard. *Fanfare*. Harper & Brothers: New York, 1957.

Rhodes, Eric. *History of the Cinema.* Hill and Wang: New York, 1976.

Riis, Jacob. *How the Other Half Lives.* Harvard University Press: Cambridge, Massachusetts, 1970 (originally published 1890).

Sann, Paul. *The Lawless Decade.* Crown: New York, 1957.

Schary, Dore. *Heyday: An Autobiography.* Little, Brown: Boston, 1980.

Schuster, Mel. *Motion Picture Performers: A Bibliography of Magazine & Periodical Articles.* Scarecrow Press: Metuchen, New Jersey, 1976.

Seldes, Gilbert. *The Seven Lively Arts.* Sagamore Press: New York, 1957.

Solberg, Carl. *Hubert Humphrey.* W. W. Norton: New York, 1984.

Traubel, Helen and Richard G. Hubler. *St. Louis Woman.* Duell, Sloan and Pearce: New York, 1959.

Walker, Stanley. *The Night Club Era.* Frederick A. Stokes: New York, 1933.

Zolotow, Maurice. *No People Like Show People.* Random House: New York, 1951.

Index